CYRIL RAY'S
COMPLEAT
IMBIBER

№ 16

By the same author

BOOKS ON WINE AND KINDRED SUBJECTS

The Gourmet's Companion (edited, with introduction)
The Compleat Imbiber: Nos 1–12 (edited, 1956–71)
The Compleat Imbiber (second series): Nos 13–15 (edited, 1986, '89, '90)
Morton Shand's A Book of French Wines (revised and edited)
In a Glass Lightly
Lafite: The Story of Château Lafite-Rothschild
Mouton-Rothschild: The Wine, the Family, the Museum
Bollinger: Story of a Champagne
Cognac
Wine with Food (with Elizabeth Ray)
The Wines of Italy
The Wines of France
The Wines of Germany
The Complete Book of Spirits and Liqueurs
The St Michael Guide to Wine
Ray on Wine
Lickerish Limericks, with filthy pictures by Charles Mozley
The New Book of Italian Wines
Robert Mondavi of the Napa Valley
Vintage Tales (edited)
and sponsored works on Ruffino Chianti, Warre's Port,
the Bartons of Langoa and Léoville, etc

BOOKS ON OTHER SUBJECTS

Scenes and Characters from Surtees
Algiers to Austria: 78 Division in the Second World War
The Pageant of London
Merry England
Regiment of the Line: The Story of the Lancashire Fusiliers
Best Murder Stories (edited, with introduction)

CYRIL RAY'S COMPLEAT IMBIBER

Nº 16

EDITED BY CYRIL RAY

MITCHELL BEAZLEY

Cyril Ray's Compleat Imbiber Nº 16
Edited and designed by Mitchell Beazley International Ltd
Michelin House, 81 Fulham Road, London SW3 6RB

Copyright © Mitchell Beazley International Ltd 1992

A CIP catalogue record for this book is available from the British Library.

ISBN 1 85732 944 9

Executive Editor *Anne Ryland*
Editors *Jonathan Earl, Stephanie Horner, Kirsty Seymour-Ure*
Art Director *Tim Foster*

Illustrations by *Natacha Ledwidge*
Jacket illustration by *John Ward RA*
Designed by *Roger Walton Studio*

Typeset by SX Composing Ltd, Rayleigh, Essex
Origination by Mandarin Offset, Hong Kong
Printed by Bath Press, Bath, Avon

Dedicated to
Christopher Foulkes
who came to the rescue;
Pamela Vandyke Price
who suggested it
– both my successors,
Christopher as Chairman,
Pamela as President
of the
Circle of Wine Writers;
and Anne Ryland
who picked up the torch

CONTENTS

A PERSONAL NOTE

The first *Compleat Imbiber* appeared in 1956, with articles culled from the Gilbey's House Magazine of the same name, with which Cyril Ray had been associated previously. It then settled into an annual routine for twelve years, always edited by Ray, with most issues stylishly designed by Charles Hasler. Keith Waterhouse describes in his Introduction some of the ups and downs of the *Imbiber* history, and Ray always hoped that he would find another sympathetic publisher to continue what had become an absorbing task for him. Although retired some years ago from regular journalism he was always squirrelling away poems, stories, cuttings and quirky anecdotes, saying "*That* would make a good *Imbiber* piece", and commissioning authors to take a light-hearted view of eating and drinking, as well as sometimes being more serious about some aspect of the wine trade.

He was working on this edition until the last few weeks of his life, so pleased that Mitchell Beazley were to publish it.

After his death I was also pleased that they considered he had left enough material and notes for the book to go ahead, and I'm deeply grateful to them and to the friends and colleagues who have contributed.

Ray had already asked Jane Gardam and Peter Luke to write for the book, and had planned to go himself to Spain to write about the wines and the Ritz, but, alas, events overtook him, and this task has been admirably fulfilled by Andrew Henderson and Charles Hennessy. He was a longstanding and enthusiastic member of the Omar Khayyám Club and, as it is the Club's centenary this year, it seemed appropriate to ask Charles Hodgson to tell us something about the Club and its famous menus.

To the good and dear friends who have written their personal tributes to Ray, to everyone who has contributed, not least John Ward for his drawing and Keith Waterhouse for his Introduction, and to Anne Ryland and Kirsty Seymour-Ure of Mitchell Beazley, who have been so kindly in their dealings with me, my warmest thanks.

ELIZABETH RAY
June 1992

INTRODUCTION

KEITH WATERHOUSE

When Cyril Ray, in his eighty-fourth year, was finally summoned to cease his toiling in the vineyard, he left provision in his will for a Bollinger party at one of his clubs for his friends and associates, who were many. If that was his memorial, then *The Compleat Imbiber* is his monument.

This celebrated literary hamper of good food and drink (with emphasis on the drink) has had a somewhat erratic publishing history. It started life as an up-market 'freebie' magazine, produced by the firm of W. and A. Gilbey for its customers, with contributions by the likes of Raymond Postgate, A. P. Herbert, John Betjeman – and Ray ("My friends call me Ray, acquaintances call me Cyril"). With the approach of the company's centenary, Ray was asked to edit a selection of past articles, which became the pioneer hardback *Imbiber*.

Just as one drink leads to another, as the temperance pamphlets remind us, so one *Compleat Imbiber* led to another. The first twelve volumes, 1956–1971, form an unbroken run which, bought on publication, would have cost the reader a total of no more than £20.55 – one of the greatest bargains of literature. When a set was auctioned at Sotheby's in 1986, it fetched £400.

It was not until that same year, after a hiatus or hiccup of fifteen years, that the next edition of the *Imbiber* appeared. Notwithstanding the studious avoidance of a No. 13 on its cover, this thirteenth issue was not an overwhelming success – "abject flop" was the phrase used by its editor, its new publishers evidently having decided that if a good wine needs no bush (or no push, as Ray, with his love of wordplay, amended the saying) then a good book on wine needs no advertising or promotion, and not much effort in the way of distribution. Only 2,750 copies were sold out of a print run of 6,000, the rest being remaindered. So *The New Compleat Imbiber*, as it was styled, is itself a collector's item of a kind.

We then had to wait until 1990 for No. 14, with which it was intended to resume the anthology's annual appearance. This, with another change of publisher and with an introduction by Kingsley Amis, went down smoothly enough. With No. 15, however, the *Imbiber – Cyril Ray's Compleat Imbiber* as it was now called – hit the rocks again. "A rogue issue" was how Ray himself described it. In an apologetic letter to contributors he wrote that when a friend brought a copy of the book to his notice, it was the first he had seen of it since handing over the material fifteen months previously. "I saw no proofs: the excellent material is marred, now that it is in print, by egregious howlers . . ." The book had appeared in the unseasonable month of March and was being neither advertised nor reviewed. Its editor, in short, disowned it: the only good news was that the firm of Mitchell Beazley had now come to the rescue and so at last, with No. 16, the *Imbiber* would once again find itself in safe harbour.

So it has proved – although the Helmsman, alas, is not here to see it. What regrettably seems likely to be the final edition of the *Imbiber*, however, bears the Ray imprint every bit as recognisably as that first edition back in 1956. By the time of his last illness Ray had got most of the material together and had annotated much of it with his pithy editorial notes; it fell to his wife Elizabeth Ray, who of course herself knows a thing or two about food and wine, to garner the remaining text. The volume as completed is as he would have sent it to the press.

"*The Compleat Imbiber*", says its publicity material, "is an institution." So was its founding editor. A socialist who kept an apartment in Albany and sent his son to Eton, who bought his boots from Lobb's and his champagne from Waitrose, a great joiner of clubs who was also a great resigner from journals on points of principle, a connoisseur of fine wines who liked nothing so much as a nice glass of Guinness, a loather of warmongering with a passion for regimental history, Cyril Ray was not in the least the bundle of contradictions some of his contemporaries teasingly made him out to be, but a compendium of the decent values. He liked the good things of life and wanted to see them better distributed.

Ray, a formidably experienced newspaperman (*Manchester Guardian*, BBC war correspondent, *Sunday Times* Moscow correspondent) came to wine writing casually, as just one of the many assignments that were tossed his way at a time of twelve-page newspapers with accordingly slimline staffing. Using his highly developed reporting skills to master his subject, he could equally well have become an expert on antique glass or 18th-century paintings had his masters demanded it of him (they probably did, and he probably was).

He made no great claims for his palate: his art was in knowing how to do his homework and then setting down the results of his researches with wit and clarity. His obituary in *The Times* records that after a dinner with distinguished wine writers of the calibre of Hugh Johnson, where many equally distinguished bottles were consumed, Ray began his speech with the words, "Many of those here have a much better palate than I, but I'm the best bloody journalist in the room by a long chalk." There were, *The Times* notes, no dissenters.

It was his matter-of-fact approach, his lack of awe (though not of respect) for wine and winemakers, his deflation of wine snobbery and his refusal to have anything to do with the descriptive tosh that blights so much wine writing – all this plus an elegant yet easy style – that made him so accessible to ignoramuses on the subject such as myself. One of the tests of a piece of good writing is whether its author can grab and hold the audience's interest in a topic they may not know the first thing about. John Arlott, for example – no stranger to these volumes – could always ensnare me with his cricket reports and ramblings, for all that I am possibly the only Yorkshireman whose knowledge of cricket could be encompassed on one side of a cigarette card. Cyril Ray had that same knack, not only as a writer but as an editor. That (discounting those two unlucky numbers!) was one of the ingredients of the *Imbiber*'s success – he chose his contributors, and selected from the authors on his shelves, not only on the basis of their expertise (that's if they had any – you needed only your writer's credentials to qualify for inclusion, which is why I come to have appeared three times in all, including this Introduction), but on their readability.

What, then, has this sixteenth *Imbiber* in store for its devotees?

The doyen himself is here, of course, with one dissertation on 1989 claret and another on Mouton; plus appreciations and tributes to him from several old friends and colleagues; plus his own observations and asides and aperçus on other contributions. These include Francatelli on serving wines, David Lipsey on Burgundy, Charles Hodgson on the Omar Khayyám Club, Deirdre McQuillan on samphire gathering, Michael Broadbent on Great Tastings – but see table of contents for groaning table of fare.

There is also a mind-blowing hangover cure from the late Peter Langan, who would have been a good writer as well as a great restaurateur if he had ever stayed sober enough to see the typewriter keys. I once suggested that he should compile his own anthology – Peter Langan's Book of Drunks – and he was seriously thinking about it when he set himself on fire. It would have been an easy collection to put together (I keep trying to unload the idea on Jeffrey Bernard): everyone has at least one good drunk story.

But over-imbibing would not be encouraged by the Great Imbiber. He had too much respect for good food and drink to see either abused. I first encountered Ray at the *Punch* table when he was that then august organ's wine correspondent – later he was to become Mr Punch's honorary wine steward. We lunched or dined regularly and when some of us grew disenchanted with the revamped *Punch*, which had set itself on a kamikaze course to rival *Viz*, we would meet at the '*Punch* Writers in Exile' table which assembled at the Garrick Club. Ray loved that kind of wheeze. It would not have surprised him to know that he was to pre-decease the ailing magazine by only a few months. He would have been aghast to learn that the celebrated table is now covered with glass, presumably to stop the marketing vandals from carving their initials in it. At least they didn't use smoke-tinted plastic.

I drag in *Punch* because *The Compleat Imbiber* is all that the 150-year-old weekly, in its heyday, strove to be – civilized, agreeable, amusing yet abrasive, and a magnet for the best writing of the day (and, in the *Imbiber's* case, of yesterday). Now, with this edition, *The Compleat Imbiber* too looks set to be consigned to the library shelf of history. Savour it while you may.

THE ART OF DINING

THE ART OF DINING

Gourmand simply means one who eats to indulge his taste, his appetite. It must be confined to those whose eating is ruled solely by their natural craving for food, and may, without injustice, be translated as 'eater'.

A *gourmet*, on the other hand, is one who tastes finely. He nibbles at things and cultivates a finicky delicacy of taste that revolts at the gross appetite of the *gourmand*. The English word *epicure* is more applicable to him than to the *gourmand*, but it does not really define him in all his glory. The *gourmet* will abstain from well-prepared food for which he may have a natural liking, on the ground that such food is not in season, or that it has been prepared in some way that violates the canons of good cookery as he understands them. He regulates his life by conventions of taste, and the vagaries in which he indulges are often as absurd as those of the faddist. For the *gourmet* is essentially a faddist – a faddist in matters of taste. An epicure is one who, while allowing taste to guide him in most things, and while condemning the indiscriminate indulgence of the *gourmand*, pays somewhat greater attention to dietetic rules, and eats his meals not according to stereotyped conventions, but with a careful selective activity that has won him the praise of all great cooks . . . The French adopted it, and put into it a meaning which it originally never aspired to, quite different from the meaning of the word *gourmand*, of which the English equivalent is one who gormandises. "It is certainly odd," [Walker] adds, "that Englishmen should have such an exalted idea of the sense of taste that they bestow its name upon the faculty of estimating all that is most sublime and beautiful in Nature and art, while they have no name left for the fine appreciation of food, for the enjoyment of the table, for the divine art of banqueting, which does not confuse dining with gorging and the gratification of the palate with the repletion of a sot."

It was left to Walker to coin such a word, and although it is perhaps not the most felicitous that could have been invented, it must stand for want of a better. He suggested the name *gastrosoph* for the supreme expert of the table, the cardinal of diners, the culmination of good taste and common-sense in the art of dining. The gastrosoph is neither a *gourmand* nor a *gourmet*. He is a person who has carefully studied dietetics and the art of eating, who pays the greatest attention to the general principles, and at the same time allows himself the widest latitude in applying them to his habits of dining. He is the dietetic artist, the expert who knows how to eat, when to eat, and what to eat; who never permits convention to interfere with his appreciation of a tasty and wholesome dish, and who despises the dictates of fashion that attempt to make him sit down to a meal that he cannot relish, or drink champagne when he prefers beer. He can appreciate vegetarian cookery when it is good, just as much as he can mixed cookery; he can abstain from caviare when it is dry and hard without a pang, and dine off a Spanish onion, a bit of Parmesan cheese and black bread when he feels the inclination to do so. His dietetic life is ruled and regulated by moderation, sanity, discrimination, and controlled taste, not by arbitrary maxims laid down by authorities. He is the ideal that every diner should strive to attain to. For dietetics should be gastrosophy, the science and art of minding one's belly very studiously, of which Dr Johnson was not ashamed to declare himself a disciple.

Extract from LIEPOLDT, *The Belly Book* (1936)

Give me King Edward (VII) for English tastes. He liked very simple food, plainly cooked, and nothing sloppy that would spoil his shirt front.

ROSA LEWIS

IN PARTIBUS INFIDELIUM

SIMON MURRAY

In 1960 19-year-old Simon Murray enlisted in the French Foreign Legion and kept a diary throughout his five-year service. He begins his military career with the instruction batallion at Mascara (Morocco), otherwise known for its wine and olive oil. The following is his account of his first meal as a Légionnaire:

The outgoing company which we will replace and which will now be sent as reinforcements to the various regiments is still here awaiting final exit. Their presence is symbolic of what we will look like in a few months' time – we hope. In contrast to us they are like a herd of young bullocks just kept from stampeding by an intangible discipline. Their morale is good and they create the impression of a force of enthusiasm and vibrance. They are continually on the move, running or assembling in small, neat, crisp-looking squads, or marching with their heads up and with their arms swinging like hell. They are in harmony in all their movements and this effect is heightened by the singing of these marvellous songs which one can hear constantly throughout the day. These men look fit and strong and quite unstoppable, like fast-moving tanks. We, *les bleux*, are spectators, non-participants, waiting for them to clear out so that we can get on stage. We have no camaraderie, no morale, no songs and we can do nothing. There is a sort of nervous tension in our ranks. It is difficult to relax and there is an edge in one's relationship with everybody else. We are perhaps all too preoccupied with number one at the moment, ensuring we do the right thing and that we keep a low profile. We need time.

At the evening meal, '*la soupe*', the old hands showed their form and one realized fully then how new we were and how far we had to go. We were all lined up outside the *réfectoire* and on the blast of a whistle the disciplined column filed in. There were long tables laden with food, along the side of which were small square metal stools, all in straight lines – perfect precision. Each man entered, removing his kepi as he did so, and stood to attention in front of his stool. Complete silence, absolute order, rigid discipline. The numbers were right, nobody was left wandering around looking for a place. The corporal entered last and called for a song, "*La tone*". A single voice broke the silence with the first few bars, at the end of which he yelled "*Trois*" and the old hands in silence counted four imaginary paces and then with a crash like a pistol-shot in a tunnel they yelled "*Quatre*" and blasted into "*La Légion Marche*". In the enclosed *réfectoire* it was like being in a cathedral with sixteen choirs going for their lives – deafening and fantastic – tremendously strong and impressive. The song finished and the corporal yelled, "*Asseyez-vous. Bon appétit!*" and with a mighty roar of "*Merci, caporal*" we dived into the food, shovelling it into our faces with gusto as fast as we could, all mixed up together. The food was good: artichokes, egg mayonnaise, beefsteak, salad, cheese, all washed down with mugs of rough Mascara wine. There was a crescendo of conversation periodically checked by screams from the corporal of "*Un peu de silence*". Everybody would start whispering and then the babble gathered momentum again and the cycle was completed by another frantic yell from the corporal.

There are a number of rules that are learned quickly in the *réfectoire*. The first is never to accept the offer of someone else's artichoke. This is fatal because while you are plucking away at the leaves the other fellow is scoffing your beefsteak and by the time you have waded through your own artichoke and his, the rest of the dishes have been licked clean.

The second rule is not to put your feet on the bar of the stool. Feet will remain at all times on the floor and the penalty for forgetting this is severe; the corporal comes up silently behind you and gives you a sharp rabbit punch on the back of the neck as you are about to swallow a mouthful of wine. It is a very nasty experience indeed and you only need one lesson to remember it a lifetime.

Extract from *Legionnaire* (1978)

START HER ON CHAMPAGNE, BOY

A. P. HERBERT

Start her on champagne, boy, but break her in to hock –
That's the only rule of life that's steady as a rock.
I've seen so many promising entanglements decline
'Cos the lady weren't contented with a nice still wine.

> *Start her on champagne, boy, but break her in to hock;*
> *And the longer you leave it the bigger is the shock.*
> > *I used to say to Liz,*
> > *"Now, what about some fizz?*
> > *Or shall we have a nice glass of hock?"*
> *I told her the history, the mystery of hock,*
> *I told her that hock would go sweetly with her frock,*
> *How the felon at the block as a rule demanded hock,*
> > *And other things with which I needn't trouble'ee;*
> *And "Hock," said she, "would do very well for me";*
> *And I said, "Waitah! a bottle of 53!"*
>
> > *And then, I don't know why –*
> > *Was it something in her eye? –*
> > *In a minute I'd be ordering the bubbly.*

If a lady chooses lobster when there's plaice at one-and-ten
It's a strain upon the passions of the tenderest of men.
Give her dinner *à la carte* when your romance has just begun,
But if love is to be lasting stick to *table d'hôte*, my son.

Start her in the stalls, boy, but train her to the pit;
Educate them up until they don't care where they sit.
*   I've done with Lizzie, boy,*
*   For her tastes were too Savoy,*
*   And mine were more Soho, I must admit.*
I told her of the cooking and the quaintness of Soho,
I told her to Soho all the clever people go,
I told her that Soho was the haunt of the beau
*   And the beginning of innumerable marriages;*
And "Soho!" she'd declare, "I'll be happy anywhere,"
And I'd say, "Splendid! Well, a bus goes there";

*   And then, I don't know why –*
*   Was it something in her eye? –*
We'd be driving in a motor-cab to Claridge's.

FRANCATELLI'S INSTRUCTIONS FOR THE SERVICE OF WINES

The judicious service of wines at the dinner-table is essential to the complete success of a well-ordered and *recherché* dinner; for on the manner and order in which this service is conducted will chiefly depend the more or less favourable judgment awarded (independently of their real claims to superiority) to the wines put before the guests.

First, let it be remembered that all possible care should be taken in removing the bottles from their bins, and afterwards also, in handling them for the purpose of drawing the corks, and decanting the wines, not to disturb any deposit that may exist in the bottles, for that deposit, if shaken, destroys not only the brilliancy of the wine, but impairs its flavour and *bouquet*.

The different kinds of Sherries, Ports, Madeira, and all Spanish and Portuguese wines in general, are the better for having been decanted several hours before being drunk. During winter their aroma is improved by the temperature of the dining-room acting upon their volatile properties for an hour or so before dinner-time. By paying due attention to this part of the process, all the mellowness which good wines acquire by age, predominates to the delight of the epicure's grateful palate. The lighter wines, such as Bordeaux, Burgundy, and most of the wines of Italy, should be most carefully handled, and decanted an hour only before dinner-time. In winter, the decanters should be either dipped in warm water or else placed near the fire, to warm them, for about ten minutes previously to their being used. In summer, use the decanters without warming them, as the genial warmth of the atmosphere will be all-sufficient, not only to prevent chilling the wines, but to develop their fragrant *bouquet*. Moreover, let these, and all delicate wines, be brought into the dining-room as late as may be consistent with convenience.

And now, as regards the order in which wines should be served during dinner: – I would recommend all *bon vivants* desirous of testing and thoroughly enjoying a variety of wines, to bear in mind that they should be drunk in the following order: viz. –

When it happens that oysters preface the dinner, a glass of Chablis or Sauterne is their most proper accompaniment: genuine old Madeira, or East India Sherry, or Amontillado, proves a welcome stomachic after soup of any kind, – not excepting turtle, – after eating which, as you value your health, avoid all kinds of punch – especially Roman punch. During the service of fish, cause any of the following to be handed round to your guests: – Amontillado, Hock, Tisane Champagne, Pouilly, Meursault, Sauterne, Arbois, vin de Grave, Montrachet, Château-Grillé, Barsac, and generally all kinds of dry white wines.

With the entrées, any of the following wines may be introduced: viz. –

BORDEAUX

Saint Julien
Leoville
Laroze
Haut-Brion
Château-Lafitte
Château-Margaux
Mouton-Lafitte
Latour
Médoc
Saint Emilion
Saint Estèphe

BURGUNDY, &c

Macon
Moulin-à-vent
Thorins
Beaune
Chassagne
Pale and brown Sherries
Amontillado
Bucellas
Mancinillo

SECOND-COURSE WINES
RED WINES

Pommard
Volnay
Nuits
Richebourg
Clos-Vougeot
Romanée-Conti
Chambertin
Saint Georges
Pouilly
Meursault
Saint Perray

Rhenish wines (red)
Ermitage
Hermitage
Tavel
Roussillon
Château neuf du Pape
Côte-rôtie
Jurançon
Monté-Fiascone
Monté-Pulciano
Vino di Pasta

WHITE WINES

Vin de Grave	Aï pétillant
Sauterne	Carbonnieux
Barsac	Champagnes
Langon	

RED CHAMPAGNES

Bouzy	Champagne
Versy	Sillery
Volnay mousseux	Sparkling Moselle
Veuve Cliquot	

DESSERT WINES

Muscat-Frontignan	Madeira
Muscat-Lunel	Malmsey Madeira
Muscat-Rivesalte	Syracuse
Grenache	Tokay
Vin de paille	Constance
Malaga	Carcavallos
Rota	Picoli
Alicante	Schiras

A question of the highest importance, but into which I may but briefly enter, is to determine to which of all these wines a decided preference should be given, both with regard to taste, and also in respect to their influence on the health of different temperaments. It is easier to settle the latter part of the question than the former, inasmuch as it is difficult, not to say impossible, to lay down rules for the guidance of the palate. Thus there are some who delight in the perfumed yet austere *bouquet* of Bordeaux, while others prefer the delicate fragrance of Champagne; some give the palm to the generous and mirth-inspiring powers of Burgundy; while the million deem that Madeira (when genuine), Port, and Sherry, from what are termed their generous natures, ignoring the plentiful admixture of alcohol, are the only wines worthy of notice. All these tastes are no doubt well enough founded on good and sufficient reasons, and may prove safe indicators for the preservation of health: – for instance, a person of sanguine temperament feels a necessity for a light sapid wine, such as *genuine* Champagnes and Rhenish wines; while the phlegmatic seek those of a more spirituous, generous nature – Burgundy, Port, Madeira, or Sherry. Those who are a prey to spleen – lowness of spirits – melancholy – are prone to select, as a sure and pleasant remedy for their frightful ailments, the wines of Italy, Spain, Portugal, Roussillon, and Burgundy. The bilious, who generally are blessed with a good appetite, provided always that they do not smoke, require a generous wine, which, while capable of acting both as an astringent and a dissolvent of the bile, is of facile digestion; such are the properties of all first-class Bordeaux wines. Bordeaux is said to be a cold wine; this false notion arises out of mere prejudice – nothing can be more contrary to truth: this health-restoring wine, as I have already stated, is of easy digestion, and possesses, moreover, the advantage of being very considerably less inebriating than any other first-class wine. In short, Burgundy is exciting, Champagne is captious, Roussillon restorative, and Bordeaux stomachic.

It now remains to show the order in which the several sorts of wines, enumerated above, should be served at table. Custom and fashion have ever had more to do with the practice than any real consideration for health or taste.

It is generally admitted by *real gourmets*, that red wines should precede the introduction of white wines, – those recommended as proper accompaniments to oysters and fish excepted. The custom most in vogue at the best tables in London and Paris is, to commence by introducing, simultaneously with the entrées, any of the follow-ing Burgundy wines: – Avallon, Coulanges, Tonnerre, Vermanton, Irancy, Mercurey, Chassagne, and, generally, all those wines known under the specific names of Macon and Auxerre: these may be varied and replaced by other wines, denominated Saint Denis, Saint Ay, and Beaugency: these again lead to the further libations of Beaune, Pommard, Volnay, Richebourg, Chambertin, Saint Georges, Roma-née. With the second course, roasts and dressed vegetables, and savoury *entremets*, honour your guests by graciously ushering to their notice sparkling Champagne and Moselle, the deliciously per-fumed Cumières, the brilliant Sillery, the glorious Hermitage, Côte-rôtie, and Château-Grillé.

With the service of the *entremets de douceur* – or, as we have it, the sweets – let iced-creaming, sparkling Champagne or Moselle be handed round; but far superior to them, I would recommend a trial of Aï *pétillant*, Arbois, Condrieux, Rivesaltes, Malaga, Frontignan, Grenache, Malmsey, Madeira, and East India Sherry.

So little wine is drunk at dessert in this country, that it would be superfluous to enter into particulars about the service further than to refer the reader to the list of wines appropriated to this part of a dinner. And what shall be said with respect to the class of wines best adapted to make their appearance on the table after dinner? Why simply this; if you have done reasonable honour to some of the good things which I will suppose your table to have been supplied with, pray let the wine alone for the present, and order up the coffee – *hot, strong,* and *bright!* Let it be made with pure – picked overland Mocha, – fresh roasted pale – coarsely ground, – and pray do forbid your housekeeper to clarify it with egg; but tell her to use a bit of genuine Russian isinglas, not the spurious filth made from all sorts of abominations, and sold at most Italian warehouses under the name of isinglas. The Cafetière à la Dubelloy, or one of Adams' Percolators, is best adapted for making good coffee without the trouble or necessity for clarifying it. And as to liqueurs? Try Eau de vie d'Andaye, Eau de la Grande Chartreuse, or ten-year-old Cognac.

Before I take my leave of you, dear reader, let me here acknowledge how much I feel indebted to the press generally for the flattering notices of my 'Cook's Guide,' which in a great measure through such favourable introduction has, in the short space of six months, gone through three large editions.

And as I now write at 'the wee hour beyont the twal,' as the Scots say, and we have entered on a new year, I will wish you all good fortune, and that you may possess the means of enjoying the delectable wines we have passed in review, and a dinner dressed by an Aberlin, a Brûnet-Montrose, a Jules Magdelin, a Georges Comte, a Sédille, or a Valentin: – and then, indeed, you will be of the most fortunate on this globe.

Extract from C. E. FRANCATELLI, *The Modern Cook* (1862)

THE BUTLER'S DUTIES

SAMUEL AND SARAH ADAMS

TO MANAGE FOREIGN WINES

The principal object to be attended to in the management of foreign wine vaults, is to keep them of a temperate heat. Care must be taken, therefore, to close up every aperture or opening, that there may be no admission given to the external air. The floor of the vault should likewise be well covered with saw-dust, which must not be suffered to get too dry and dusty, but must receive now and then an addition of new, lest, when bottling or racking wine, some of the old dust should fly into it. At most vaults, in the winter, it is necessary to have a stove or chafing-dish, to keep up a proper degree of warmth. In the summer time it will be best to keep them as cool as possible.

To Fit up a Cellar of Wines and Spirits

Provide a good rope and tackling, to let down the casks into the vault or cellar, and a slide; ladder, or pulley for casks to slide or roll on.

A pair of strong slings

A pair of can hooks and a pair of crate hooks

A large wooden funnel

Two or three copper funnels from a quart to a gallon each

Two racking cocks

Two wine bottling cocks

A brace and various bits

Two small tubs

A square basket to hold the corks

Two small tin funnels

A small strainer

Two corkscrews

Two or three baskets

A whisk to beat the finings

Three flannel or linen bags

A strong iron screw to raise the bungs

A pair of pliers

Bungs, corks, and vent pegs

Two frets or middle sized gimblets

A block of wood to put under the pipes when topping them over in a narrow passage, or in casing them

A small valinch to taste wine

A crane, and a small copper pump to rack off

Two or three gallon cans, made of wood

Some sheet lead and tacks to put on broken staves

Brown paper to put round cocks and under the lead, when stopping leaks

A staff with a chain at one end to rumage the wines, &c.

Shots and lead canister, or bristle brush, and two cloths to wash bottles

Two large tubs

Some small racks that will hold six dozen each

A cooper's adze

An iron and a wooden driver to tighten hoops

Two dozen of wooden bungs of different sizes

A thermometer, which is to be kept in the vault, a stove or chafing-dish, to keep the heat of the vault to a known temperature

A few dozen of delf labels

A cupboard to hold all the tools

A spade, two good stiff birch brooms, and a rake to level the saw-dust.

To rack Foreign Wines

The vault of cellar should be of a temperate heat, and the casks sweet and clean. Should they have an acid or musty smell, it may be remedied by burning brimstone matches in them; and if not clean, rinse them well out with cold water, and after draining rinse with a quart of brandy, putting the brandy

afterwards into the ullage cask. Then strain the lees or bottoms through a flannel or linen bag. But put the bottoms of port into the ullage cask without going through the filtering bag. In racking wine that is not on the stillage, a wine-pump is desirable.

To manage and improve poor Red Port

If wanting in body, colour and flavour, draw out thirty or forty gallons, and return the same quantity of young and rich wines. To a can of which put three gills of colouring, with a bottle of wine or brandy. Then whisk it well together, and put it into the cask stirring it well. If not bright in about a week or ten days, fine it for use; previous to which put in at

different times a gallon of good brandy. If the wine is short of body, put a gallon or two of brandy in each pipe, by a quart or two at a time, as it feeds the wine better than putting it in all at once. But if the wines are in a bonded cellar, procure a funnel that will go to the bottom of the cask, that the brandy may be completely incorporated with the wine.

To manage Claret

Claret is not a wine of a strong body, though it requires to be of a good age before it is used, and, therefore, it should be well managed; the best method is to feed it every two or three weeks with a pint or two of French brandy. Taste it frequently, to know what state it is in, and use the brandy accordingly, but never put much in

at a time, while a little incorporates with the wine, and feeds and mellows it.

If the claret is faint, rack it into a fresh-emptied hogshead, upon the lees of good claret; and bung it up, putting the bottom downwards for two or three days, that the lees may run through it.

To recover pricked Foreign Wines

Take a bottle of red port that is pricked, add to it half an ounce of tartarised spirit of wine, shake the liquor well together, and set it by for a few days, and it will be found much altered for the better. If this operation be dexterously performed, pricked wines may be absolutely recovered by it, and remain saleable for some time; and the same method may be used to malt liquors just turned sour.

To manage Hermitage and Burgundy

Red hermitage must be managed in the same way as claret, and the white likewise, except the colouring, which it does not require. Burgundy should be managed in the same manner as red hermitage.

To manage Lisbon Wine

If the Lisbon is dry, take out of the pipe thirty-five or forty gallons, and put in the same quantity of calcavella, stir it well about, and this will make a pipe of good mild Lisbon: or, if it be desired to convert mild into dry, take the same quantity out as above mentioned, before, and fill the pipe with Malaga sherry, stirring it about as the other. The same kind of fining used for Vidonia will answer for Lisbon wines; or it may be fined with the whites and shells of sixteen eggs, and a small handful of salt; beat it together to a froth, and mix it with a little of the wines; then pour it into the pipe, stir it about, and let it have vent for three days; after which bung it up, and in a few days it will be fine. Lisbon when bottled should be packed either in sawdust or leather in a temperate place.

To improve Sherry

If the sherry be new and hot, rack it off into a sweet cask, add five gallons of mellow Lisbon, which will take off the hot taste, then give it a head, take a quart of honey, mix it with a can of wine, and put it into the cask when racking. By this method, Sherry for present use will be greatly improved, having much the same effect upon it as age.

To improve White Wines

If the wine have an unpleasant taste, rack off one half; and to the remainder add a gallon of new milk, a handful of bay-salt, and as much rice; after which take a staff, beat them well together for half an hour, and fill up the cask, and when rolled well about, stillage it, and in a few days it will be much improved.

If the white wine is foul and has lost its colour, for a butt or pipe take a gallon of new milk, put it into the cask, and stir it well about with a staff; and when it has settled, put in three ounces of isinglass made into a jelly, with a quarter of a pound of loaf sugar scraped fine, and stir it well about. On the day following, bung it up, and in a few days it will be fine and have a good colour.

To fine a hogshead of Claret

Take the whites and shells of six fresh eggs, and proceed as with port finings. Claret requires to be kept warm in saw-dust when bottled.

To fine Port Wine

Take the whites and shells of eight fresh eggs, beat them in a wooden can or pail, with a whisk, till it becomes a thick froth; then add a little wine to it, and whisk it again. If the pipe is full take out four or five gallons of the wine to make room for the finings. If the weather be warmish, add a pint of fresh-water sand to the finings. Stir it well about; after which put in the finings, stirring it for five minutes; put in the can of wine, leaving the bung out for a few hours, that the froth may fall: then bung it up, and in eight or ten days it will be fine and fit for bottling.

To make and apply Finings

Put the finings into a can or pail, with a little of the liquor about to be fined, whisk them altogether till they are perfectly mixed, and then nearly fill the can with the liquor, whisking it well about again; after which, if the cask be full, take out four or five gallons to make room; then take the staff, and give it a good stirring; next whisk the finings up, and put them in; afterwards stir it with the staff for five minutes. Then drive the bung in, and bore a hole with a gimblet, that it may have vent for three or four days, after which drive in a vent peg.

To convert White Wine into Red

Put four ounces of turnesole rags into an earthen vessel, and pour upon them a pint of boiling water; cover the vessel close, and leave it to cool; strain off the liquor, which will be of a fine deep red inclining to purple. A small portion of this colours a large quantity of wine. This tincture may either be made in brandy, or mixed with it, or else made into a syrup, with sugar, for keeping.

In those countries which do not produce the tingeing grape which affords a blood-red juice, wherewith the wines of France are often stained, in defect of this, the juice of elderberries is used, and sometimes log-wood is used at Oporto.

To clean Wine Decanters

Cut some brown paper into very small bits, so as to go with ease into the decanters; then cut a few pieces of soap very small, and put some water, milk-warm, into the decanters, upon the soap and paper; put in also a little pearl ash; by well working this about in the decanters it will take off the crust of the wine, and give the glass a fine polish. Where the decanters have had wine left to stand in them a long time, take a small cane with a bit of sponge tied tight at one end; by putting this into the decanters any crust of the wine may be removed. When the decanters have been properly washed, let them be thoroughly dried, and turned down in a proper rack.

If the decanters have wine in them when put by, have some good corks always at hand to put in instead of stoppers; this will keep the wine much better.

To decant Wine

Be careful not to shake or disturb the crust when moving it about, or drawing the cork, particularly Port wine. Never decant wine without a wine-strainer, with some fine cambric in it, to prevent the crust, and bits of cork going into the decanter. In decanting Port wine do not drain it too near; there are generally two-thirds of a wine glass of thick dregs in each bottle, which ought not to be put in; but in white wine there is not much settling; pour it out however slowly, and raise the bottle up gradually: the wine should never be decanted in a hurry, therefore always do it before the family sit down to dinner. Do not jostle the decanters against each other when moving them about, as they easily break when full.

Extract from *The Complete Servant* (1825)

LORD PEMBROKE'S PORT WINE

JOHN TIMBS

Lord Palmerston one day related the following anecdote to a dep-utation of gentlemen, who waited upon him to urge the reduction of the wine duties. Referring to the question of adulterations, "I re-member," said his lordship, "my grandfather, Lord Pembroke, when he placed wine before his guests, said: 'There, gentlemen, is my champagne, my claret, &c. I am no great judge, and I give you this on the authority of my wine-merchant; but I can answer for my port, for I made it myself.' I have still his receipt, which I look on as a curiosity; but I confess *I have never ventured to try it.*" The follow-ing is the veritable receipt which Lord Pembroke adopted: – Eight gallons of genuine port wine, forty gallons of cider, brandy to fill the hogshead. Elder-tops will give it the proper roughness, and cochi-neal whatever strength of colouring you please. The quantity made should not be less than a hogshead. It should be kept fully two years in cask, and as long in bottle before it is used.

Extract from *A Century of Anecdote from 1760 to 1860* (1864)

BREAD AROUND THE MEDITERRANEAN

ROBIN HOWE

Bread may once again grace our tables, after many years of exile through the whim of dietary fashion – though it never left Mediterranean tables. We are now actually encouraged to eat it, though of course not any old bread. It should be an 'honest' loaf, made of good flour that has not been too highly refined, so that it still has plenty of its natural fibre, protein, calcium and vitamins of the B group. When flour has been milled and bleached beyond endurance to become deathly white, it has lost much of its value – but then, curiously, the law demands that many of the lost nutrients are returned; a strange procedure. But just as so many people prefer white rice, many insist on white bread. Even around the Mediterranean, a lot of white and off-white bread is eaten, but the latter at least is reasonably nutritious – even properly made white bread is not wholly despicable from a nutritional point of view. And the Mediterranean countries have a rich variety of traditional types of bread of all shades. Even the crustiness of good bread is of benefit to health, according to some dietitians, who attribute the Latin resistance to dental decay to the fact that their crusty loaves make their teeth and gums work harder.

For well over 7,000 years grain in one form or another has been the staple food of mankind. At first anything that could be found, such as wild millet, would have been coarsely pounded and boiled into a thick mash, and sometimes this must have accidentally dried up into a rough, unleavened loaf which was found to be more palatable. The discovery of leavening to make the bread rise was also certainly accidental. Spores of wild yeasts and other useful organisms drift around in the air or are found on the surfaces of food grains. Even today, in a place where the air is unpolluted, it is possible to 'infect' bread dough in this way. Once one batch has been leavened, if a little of the raw dough is held back and mixed with the next batch, or even if the mixing-bowl is washed less than thoroughly, the leavening can be passed on to the next batch.

Unleavened bread is still made in some of the more primitive regions, or by nomads who do not have time to bother with the niceties of bread-making. But it is heavy and indigestible, so once leavening was discovered, there was good reason to persevere with it.

The earliest evidence of leavened bread comes from the northern Balkan region. Here, many little clay models of ovens have been discovered; they may be religious offerings or toys. They depict a type of outdoor oven still used in rural areas, a beehive-shaped clay structure about a yard wide and two feet high. At one site near Stara Zagora in Bulgaria they also found a clay model of a loaf, and it must have been a representation of a leavened one, for it is round rather than flat and the clay has been pierced with many holes to indicate the spongy texture of risen bread. The date is between 5500 and 5000 BC. Real bread made there and then must have been mainly of barley, no other suitable grain being available.

The ancient Egyptians were skilled makers of leavened bread. Actual loaves have been found in tombs, preserved by the dry desert air. They are of several shapes and sizes, long, round, triangular and conical. Inscriptions and pictures tell us that professional millers and bakers were well-established by 2000 BC. In the larger establishments they kneaded the dough with their feet. The loaves in the tombs are of wheat; by this time the Egyptians had improved the primitive varieties of the plant, from which leavened bread cannot be made, into a proper bread wheat. Probably the poor seldom saw a wheat loaf and had to make do with poorer grains such as millet, which will not make a well-risen loaf.

The Greeks learned the art of bread-making from the Egyptians. They had a high regard for bread as a strength-giving food, and it was part of the recommended diet for athletes – everyone else would have eaten it anyway, of course. According to the late second-century writer Athenaeus, it was made in very hygienic conditions, and the bakers were obliged to wear gloves and a mask like a surgeon's. The Romans had large public bakehouses, and in some periods of the empire, bread was even distributed free to the people.

This free distribution set a pattern for the Italians, who have always consumed vast quantities of bread. The finest bread was of wheat flour, sieved to remove the bran so that it was more or less white: even then, white bread was in demand. This flour was called *simila*, from which our word 'semolina' comes. Pliny wrote that the quality of the bread depends on "the goodness of the wheat grains and the fineness of the sieve", but both among the Greeks and the Romans, those who could not afford fine bread made do with darker bread of barley or mixed grains of all kinds.

Among the more conservative Romans, there was a feeling that light, white bread was not 'honest' and that Romans ought to eat dark, unleavened bread as their hardy forefathers had. They reserved a special contempt for the fine bread made by the German barbarians who, being beer drinkers, did not need to raise it by the cumbersome technique of keeping back a piece from the previous batch. They simply scooped as much yeast as they wanted from a batch of fermenting beer. In this way they were able to make ultra-light bread of a kind otherwise unattainable until the modern introduction of purified, compressed yeast sold in blocks.

The distinction between the fine wheat bread for the rich and the rough bread of other grains eaten by the poor persisted for centuries. Alternative ingredients used around the Mediterranean included barley and millet; the poorest added ground beans or, in times of famine, even wild grasses; and later came maize from America, and also pumpkin, which makes quite a palatable bread when added to a cereal flour. Rye is a grain of northern regions, not the Mediterranean. Today, however, imports of inexpensive but good-quality wheat from North America have made this by far the dominant grain, and eighty per cent of the world's bread is made of it.

Bread is, and always will be, of immense importance to the peoples of Europe. In the Middles Ages a baker who baked poor bread or gave short weight could be publicly whipped, or have his ears nailed to a post, or be pilloried or dragged through the streets on a hurdle with the offending loaf hung around his neck. In Germany the life of a baker was so highly valued that the killer of one was punished three times as severely as one who had killed an ordinary man.

The two countries which have the best and most varied bread are

France and Italy: the latter may surprise some, but in reality Italian breads as a whole can stand any comparison with the better-known French ones.

Naturally, the French consider that no bread competes with theirs. To the foreigner, French bread is represented by long, thin, crisp *baguettes* and the even thinner *ficelles*, both feather-light and made of the whitest flour. The French would not deny the image, for they are most fond of these kinds and may be seen any morning (for French bakers bake even on Sundays) with half a dozen loaves under their arms, more often than not nibbling happily at the crusty ends as they walk along. In fact, you need not even ask the way to the baker's shop: just walk the opposite way to the procession and you will get there.

But these are far from being the only kinds. There are at least twenty, and most likely many more types of bread. No French baker thinks anything of baking a dozen different kinds; he does so with pride, as his kind have been doing for centuries. In 1665, Samuel Pepys noted after he had attended a meeting of the Royal Society that he had listened to a "fine discourse . . . among others, a very particular account of the making of several sorts of bread in France which is accounted the best place for bread in the world".

The French eat bread with every meal. They may start the day with *brioches*, semi-sweet rolls often referred to as 'the French breakfast bread', and one of whose airy texture French bakers are particularly proud. A large family will have a *pain de campagne*, a long, thick, crusty loaf that is part of every working-class breakfast. There are brown loaves and black rye ones, flour-dusted wheat loaves with a hard crust, and loaves of diverse shapes and sizes from *petits pains* (rolls) to massive thick, round ones. Special types include *pain brioché*, a semi-sweet bread with a rather spongy texture; spiced breads such as the *pistolet*, a small, roll-like loaf; and the popular light, crisp Vienna loaf with its slashed crust. Some bakers make fancy loaves in amusing shapes such as men and animals.

To the Italians bread is so important that it is not hard to believe that a Sicilian family of eight can demolish eight pounds daily – the bread would usually be of the soft, flat 'Arab' type. A 'poor boy's sandwich' on that island is half a long loaf, split and liberally spread with oil, tomatoes, salami, cheese, lettuce, and oregano. This is what a labourer takes with him to the fields for his midday meal.

Italian bread, too, ranges in size from tiny *panini* or rolls to huge 'housewife' loaves, as large in every way as the wheel of a small car. Some are solid discs; others have a hole in the middle that you could get your head through – huge as they are, buyers constantly come back for more. Nowhere is there greater enthusiasm for bread than in Sardinia, where the aroma of baking bread constantly strikes the nostrils in town and village alike. One peculiar kind is called *carta da musica* because it is so thin that it resembles paper on which music could be written. Excellently crisp, it is nibbled during a meal.

In country districts bread is often still made in wood-fired ovens, and simple and honest bread it is. When the bakers have made a batch they usually put up a large notice announcing that hot fresh bread is there for all to come and buy, which attracts the attention of passing motorists as well as the locals.

Italians, too, make a speciality of 'sculptured' bread moulded in fantastic shapes. The art goes back to the sixteenth century and the court at Ferrara. Even today the bread of this city is said by its inhabitants to be the finest in the world, despite any rival claims by Frenchmen past or present. One may find 'sculptured' bread here and there throughout the country. In Sicily they make not only birds and beasts, horses and carts, but also altar offerings to decorate the church on feast days. These breads are not really meant to be eaten, though they can be; often they are varnished to make them last. In Milan there is a baker who spends all his time baking sculptured bread. The same city has a Bread Club, much as one might have a Wine Club.

You would be hard to please if you could not find a bread to your liking in Italy. All you need to do is follow your nose to the nearest baker.

The Spanish are even more insistent on the freshness of bread than the French. As in many other parts of the Mediterranean, bakers bake twice a day, and the housewife goes twice daily to the *panaderia*, unless she bakes her own bread as many do. I am told that there is no surer way of irritating a Spanish husband than giving him stale bread. Bread appears at every meal, always with the *cocido*, that famous national dish. Although the Spanish have a reverence for bread which verges on the spiritual, they make full practical use of it. Any that is not eaten at once is made into a very garlicky soup, of a kind which is also made in France and Italy. This simple soup, made of bread, garlic and water, is surprisingly palatable.

When I was last in Greece the baker's boy used to come to the house where I was staying, bringing delicious sesame rolls and yelling *"freska koulouris"* as he rode up to the door on his bicycle. After his visit the house was filled with the sweet smell of hot bread. Later I would meet him delivering coarse, soft brown bread, the loaves slung haphazardly over the handlebars. On the islands, I remember the two-panniered donkeys laden with crisp bread.

In Turkey the same kinds of bread could be found. Every morning we had sesame rings or rolls, still warm from the oven, with our strong black coffee. With our kebabs and *köfte* we had *pide*, which we used to scoop up the yogurt sauce served with them. *Pide*, or *pitta* in both Greek and Arabic, or *pita* in Hebrew, is a bread which has been made in much the same way all around the eastern and southern shore of the Mediterranean since Biblical days. It is a flat, plate-shaped loaf, leavened now though it was not always so and the Bedouin still make an unleavened version. It is baked in a very hot oven so that it puffs up, and while still hot is split and filled with all kinds of savoury fillings.

In the Arab world even more than among the Spanish, bread is treated with reverence as a gift from God. There are various qualities of wheat flour from the white used to make *pitta* to coarse, dark types which make a crisper flat bread. Bread is eaten with every meal: it is used to wrap up meat, or dipped into sauces, or toasted and used as a basis for soups.

In fact from Spain in the west to Egypt in the east, and from the Alps to the Atlas mountains, there is no end to the delights of bread. It is easy to say that bread is 'the staff of life'; but around the Mediterranean this really is true.

Extract from *The Mediterranean Diet* (1985)

THE LOGICAL VEGETARIAN

G. K. CHESTERTON

*"Why shouldn't I have a purely vegetarian drink? Why shouldn't I
take vegetables in their highest form, so to speak? The modest vege-
tarians ought obviously to stick to wine or beer, plain vegetarian
drinks, instead of filling their goblets with the blood of bulls and
elephants, as all conventional meat-eaters do, I suppose."*

DALROY

You will find me drinking rum,
Like a sailor in a slum,
You will find me drinking beer like a Bavarian.
You will find me drinking gin
In the lowest kind of inn,
Because I am a rigid Vegetarian.

So I cleared the inn of wine,
And I tried to climb the sign,
And I tried to hail the constable as "Marion."
But he said I couldn't speak,
And he bowled me to the Beak
Because I was a Happy Vegetarian.

Oh, I knew a Doctor Gluck,
And his nose it had a hook,
And his attitudes were anything but Aryan;
So I gave him all the pork
That I had, upon a fork
Because I am myself a Vegetarian.

I am silent in the Club,
I am silent in the pub.,
I am silent on a bally peak in Darien;
For I stuff away for life
Shoving peas in with a knife,
Because I am at heart a vegetarian.

No more the milk of cows
Shall pollute my private house
Than the milk of the wild mares of the Barbarian
I will stick to port and sherry,
For they are so very, very,
So very, very, very Vegetarian.

From *The Flying Inn* (1914)

GUINNESS IS GOOD FOR ME . . .

Well, if it's a sin to like Guinness
Then that I admit's what my sin is:
I like it with fizz,
Or just as it is,
And it's much better for me than gin is . . .

CYRIL RAY

THE RELUCTANT HOST

KINGSLEY AMIS

FAREHAM, Herts   THE GREEN MAN
½ mile off A595   Mill End 0043

No sooner has one gone over one's surprise at finding a genuine coaching inn less than 40 miles from London – and 8 from the M1 – than one is marvelling at the quality of the equally genuine English fare (the occasional disaster apart!). There has been an inn on this site since the Middle Ages, from which parts of the present building date; after some 190 years of service as a dwelling its original function and something of its original appearance, were restored in 1961. Mr Allington will tell its story to the interested (there is, or was, at least one ghost) and be your candid guide through the longish menu. Try the eel soup (6/-), pheasant pie (15/6), saddle of mutton and caper sauce (17/6), treacle roll (5/6). Wine list short, good (except for white Burgundies), a little expensive. Worthington E, Bass, Whitbread Tankard on draught. Friendly, efficient service. No children's prices.

Cl. Su L. Must Book L; F, Sa & Su D. Meals 12.30–3; 7–10.30. Alc main dishes 12/6 to 25/-. Seats 40. Car park. No dogs. B & B from 42/6.
                                                                    Class A

App. Bernard Levin; Lord Norwich; John Dankworth; Harry Harrison; Wynford Vaughan-Thomas; Dennis Brogan; Brian W. Aldiss; and many others.

The point about white Burgundies is that I hate them myself. I take whatever my wine supplier will let me have at a good price (which I would never dream of doing with any other drinkable). I enjoyed seeing those glasses of Chablis or Pouilly Fuissé, so closely resembling a blend of cold chalk soup and alum cordial with an additive or two to bring it to the colour of children's pee, being peered and sniffed at, rolled round the shrinking tongue and forced down somehow by parties of young technology dons from Cambridge or junior television producers and their girls. Minor, harmless compensations of this sort are all too rare in a modern innkeeper's day.

.   .   .

Joyce had put up a cold collation: artichoke with a *vinaigrette*, a Bradenham ham, a tongue the chef had pressed himself, a game pie from the same hand, salads and a cheese board with radishes and spring onions. I missed out the artichoke, a dish I have always tended to despise on biological grounds. I used to say that a man with a weight problem should eat nothing else, since after each meal he would be left with fewer calories in him than he had burnt up in the toil of disentangling from the bloody things what shreds of nourishment they contained. I would speculate that a really small man, one compelled by his size to eat with a frequency distantly comparable to that of the shrew or the mole, would soon die of starvation and/or exhaustion if locked up in a warehouse full of artichokes, and sooner still if compelled besides to go through the rigmarole of dunking each leaf in *vinaigrette*. But I did not go into any of this now, partly because Joyce, who liked every edible thing and artichokes particularly, always came back with the accusation that I hated food.

This is true enough. For me, food not only interrupts everything while people eat it and sit about waiting for more of it to be served, but also casts a spell of vacancy before and after. No other sensual activity must take place at a set time to be enjoyed by anybody at all, or comes up so inexorably and so often. Some of the stuff I can stand. Fruit slides down, bread soon goes to nothing, and all pungent swallowables have a value of their own that transcends mere food. As for the rest of it, chewing away at the vile texture of meat, pulling bones out of tasteless mouthfuls of fish or encompassing the sheer nullity of vegetables is not my idea of a treat. At least sex does not demand a simultaneous outflow of talk, and drink needs no mastication.

No drinking to speak of went on at this lunch. While I tried to keep my mind entirely on my objections to food, I covered some ham and tongue with chutney and hot sauce and washed the mixture down with a powerful tumbler of whisky and water. It did not look very powerful, thanks to my use of one of those light-coloured Scotches so handy for the man who wants a stronger potion than he cares to advertise to his company. The onions and radishes got me through a small hunk of fresh Cheddar; I had made a good meal. We went on to coffee, that traditional device for prolonging artificially the conditions and atmosphere of food-consumption. I took a lot of it, not in the hope of sobering up, for coffee is no help there and I was already as sober as I could hope to be, but to render myself reasonably wakeful. I wanted to be in some sort of form for later that afternoon.

Extract from *The Green Man* (1969)

A SMALL TRIBUTE
TO A GREAT PERSONALITY

PAMELA VANDYKE PRICE

Cyril Ray was the hub of any gathering he attended. This is an analogy I think he might have appreciated: the hub, even when small, dominates the wheel.

Not only would Cyril be the centre of conversation, but he provoked good talk in others as much as he contributed to it himself. Never did he attempt to dominate, and seldom was his precise articulation reinforced by an increase in volume. Small in stature, tending to a gentle portliness in later years, slightly rubicund of complexion, beaky of nose, bright of eye, always sleek of hair and trimly attired, Cyril's presence might not immediately be registered by someone coming upon him unwittingly at a party – until the laughter around him, the buzz of conversation, his gentle flirtation with the pretty women, all indicated that here was someone special.

On many occasions I've been Cyril's guest, travelled with him and attended grand functions when he was present. But we seldom discussed wine. Personalities of the wine trade – liked, loved and loathed – yes! The history of the great establishments, certainly. We also loved to trade odd anecdotes; Cyril was like a truffle pig, hunting down amusing incidents from the past and sometimes – perhaps indiscreetly – from the present. All this made him a cornucopia of delight as a conversationalist. Not for him the lengthy and detailed descriptions of wines, many of which, by his standards, were indifferent, or even bad, pieces of writing. Wine to Cyril was one of the many good things of life, and I imagine him arguing furiously, though always courteously, with his many dear friends in the Great

Tasting Room in the Sky. Tasting, as such, he didn't enjoy: "Invite me to a simple office lunch, and let me try the wines ready to drink."

After one glitzy tasting of more than a century of vintages of Château Lafite that he'd attended in the United States, some of us rushed to him to ask whether the 1870 was holding up, and what news of the 1890s, and what about – ? "Oh, it was all very fine, but I'd rather have had, say, half a dozen of the top wines with some cold meat and salad – and *you*, Pamela, would have been sent off to a fashion show with the other women!" Not that he would ever have deprived me of what, as he realised, was my obsession and passion. But he might sit in the car while some of us went ferreting into Médoc *chais* to taste the young wines, perhaps to have a reviving snooze, or (as once occurred when on a press trip that included a lengthy session in a mineral water plant) retreat to an outdoor café and compose one of his witty limericks.

Stories about Cyril will proliferate. Once, at an impressive dinner at Mouton-Rothschild, Cyril leaned across the exquisite table setting to enquire "Don't you think, Monsieur le Baron, that the term 'Mouton Cadet' is something of a misnomer?" (He didn't quite say "passing off".)

In 1960 Cyril, with another friend in the wine trade, came with me to the sixtieth birthday luncheon for the late Allan Sichel at Château Grand-Puy-Lacoste. All the wines served were of the 1900 vintage, and although the French guests enthused about the 'porto' served, some of us, including Cyril, went round the table after the host had left the salon and lapped up the remnants of the 1900 Cognac that had been left in a number of glasses.

Often Cyril would pour me "a glass of fizz" at Albany. Or I'd telephone: "Cyril, you know *everything* – who said, who did, who wrote, who was –" and the little deprecatory cough and laugh, "*Dear* Pamela –", and off we'd go. If a definition was required, there'd be a thunder of dictionaries pulled from shelves in the background. If some fact had to be verified, he'd ring me back – he was, always, 'absolute for truth'. I delighted in his tales of the past, such as that of William Stone, 'the Squire of Piccadilly', who'd lived at Albany to a great age and once asked Cyril "Young man – what do boys do these days about gels – y'know – are there plenty of decent 'houses'?" To which Cyril demurely replied "My dear Willie, I think these days young people arrange things between themselves." "What d'yer mean? Chaps sleepin' with other chaps' sisters? Disgustin'!" And Cyril would report the dropped 'g's and intonations of pre-1914 voices as few actors can these days. One thing puzzled us. Why, when Bertrand Russell, as a youth, was entertaining Gladstone, and the ladies had left the table, did the Grand Old Man murmur "This is very good port they've given me – but why did they serve it in a claret glass?" Many were our theories about this – and now Cyril will be able to ask directly . . .

On graver subjects, such as warfare, Cyril could be spellbinding. He seldom spoke about his own achievements – constant courage, impeccable reporting – but he would expatiate on great campaigns, "although I'm not strong on those of Alexander". We'd discuss why Napoleon couldn't ride throughout the day of Waterloo (his problem was piles), or what went wrong with Soult in the Peninsular campaign. Was Gettysburg more significant than Waterloo? Why did Ney opt for trial by court martial . . . ?

As a don, Cyril would have driven generations of students to adoration or exasperation. He insisted on everything being checked; he might not find your arguments acceptable, but he respected you for marshalling facts against him.

The last time I saw him was when, with another dear colleague, we visited him at Albany before an extra-special tasting at Spencer House, to be followed by dinner. Both of us were '*en grande tenue*'. Cyril, though becoming fragile after long and recurrent illness, greeted us formally, and, offering us a drink, commented that we looked "very splendid". He escorted us to the door. Later I telephoned to describe what was an historic occasion – wonderful wines, fairy-tale surroundings, the staff enjoying our pleasure, the hosts quietly delighting in the superlative 'party' they had created and the guests almost awed (but not quite, for we were all articulate writers) by the coming-together of so many of the gracious things of life. And Cyril shared a few giggles with me about it too.

He could be dogmatic, difficult (once he and I didn't speak for six months), and his problems with publishers could make a book. He could not understand inefficiency and he, the journalist whose copy *had* to be sent in on time, never began to appreciate the delays that occur in the publication of a book. He never accepted that facts are not always checked, must have felt that distortions of English were a sort of sacrilege, and couldn't tolerate sloppiness in the use of words, or the affectations of writers who don't actually live by what they earn from their writing. As a journalist and – had it not been for the Second World War – an historian, he made both a life and a personality that a wide variety of people enjoyed and respected. Many who have written tributes to him have admitted that he would have corrected their copy – for the better. I go on missing him, for I loved him. He is irreplaceable – and he was always *fun*.

TOUR DE FRANCE

GOOD BURGUNDY IS RARE: GREAT BURGUNDY RAREST

DAVID LIPSEY

How can anyone love burgundy? It is made, the red variety, from a grape, the pinot noir, which defies successful cultivation anywhere. The climate in Burgundy, north of Lyon, is too cold for it. The vineyards have been divided and subdivided by French inheritance laws so some yield barely enough juice to satisfy a gnat's thirst.

Burgundy has spawned its fair share of incompetent winemakers and more than its fair share of avaricious and mendacious ones. Burgundy costs too much. It takes five, ten, fifteen years for the wine to mature. After five, ten, fifteen years, you may uncork to find the dreaded grey rot; or the nasty taste that results from hailstorms; or, only too frequently, a pale insipidity which comes from overcropping. In truth, most burgundy tastes nasty, brutish and short. Anyone with a taste for good wine and an ounce of common sense will turn to Australia, or (if they be unshakable in their Francophilia) to Bordeaux; and leave burgundy to the dupes.

All this is true, horribly true. Yet it discomforts the true burgundy lover not a jot. We burgundy lovers are not the easy come, easy go type. Not for us casual pick-ups, nor one-night stands. Our passion is a grand one. We let it smoulder long. We defer its gratification. We shrug aside disappointment; indeed, the disappointment that is our lot serves only to inflame our devotion to still greater heights.

Our senses are inflamed by oenological pornography. We scour Michael Broadbent's *Great Vintage Wine Book* for what he has to say of the finest and the rarest of the wines: of Grands-Echézeaux '49 and Richebourg '59 and the '61 Chambertin. We look to see which have won marks in the nineties, or, miracle of miracles, 100 out of 100, from Robert Parker, whose new book, *Burgundy*, is the most comprehensive guide through the minefield. But pornography is all it is. We know, even as we read, that these treasures are not for

us. Most such bottles have long since been drunk. Those that have
not lie deep in the cellars of fellow addicts, and cannot be bought for
love or money – of which, in any case, they would require a sum
beyond Croesus. Even if we got them, they would probably turn out
to be badly stored, or over the top, or simply not as good as they
were cracked up to be.

Even the pornography can turn out to be a little perverted. This is
how Anthony Hanson, author of *Burgundy*, describes the wine's
nose:

"Great Burgundy smells of shit. It is most surprising, but the
French recognised it long ago, *ça sent la merde* and *ça sent le purin*
being common expressions of the Côte."

It does not sound exactly encouraging. It would not tempt the
average claret drinker. But the true burgundy lover knows what he
means. A whiff even of inadequate pinot noir bears a tantalising hint
of what decent pinot noir must smell like – concentrated essence of
the farmyard.

Good burgundy is rare. Great burgundy is rarest. Most burgundy
lovers will be lucky to taste the former once or twice a year; and the
latter perhaps never. Yet it makes no difference. The hint in the
lesser is enough to convey the promise of the greater. The search
goes on, the Holy Grail beckons, and while the taste buds have life
left in them, the quest will never be abandoned.

I have now been in thrall to the passion for nine years. My father
died, bequeathing me a cellar of very decent claret, and a bottle of
Louis Latour's Savigny-lès-Beaune 1972, bought from a friend. This
is a quite good year and Savigny-lès-Beaune a quite good commune,
but its reputation is not half as elevated as most of the claret in the
collection. Never mind; one sniff and I was done. The modest bottle
summoned up the ideal image of the great bottle. May my beloved
father's memory forgive me, but the claret has been sold at auction,
and the proceeds reinvested in the quest for the perfect burgundy.

The odds are formidable. Buy fine claret and you have the classification of 1855 to help you. No doubt some fourth growths ought
really to be thirds and a few seconds; and vice versa. But you can be
pretty sure that a decent château in a decent year will produce a
decent bottle.

Not so with burgundy. One works in multiple dimensions. The

vineyard matters. On average, a *premier cru* will be better than a village wine and a *grand cru* better than a *premier cru*, but with many exceptions. Corton, a *grand cru*, yields much rubbish; ditto, Clos de Vougeot. Everywhere there are traps; names that look like *premier cru* names, but are, in fact, meaningless *lieux-dits*. Then again, some *lieux-dits* beat the *premiers crus*. The revered Domaine de la Romanée-Conti sometimes decides to bar wine writers who dare say that in this vintage, or from that *clos*, the emperor wears no clothes; yet the writers are being no more than honest.

Vintages of course matter, particularly in this climate. But the exceptions keep on popping up. There is probably no good 1975 red burgundy, and precious little 1984, but 1987, initially talked down, has yielded me the best bottle of the year, a Vosne-Romanée by Méo-Camuzet.

Then – and this is the element that it is fashionable to talk up – there is the matter of who owns the particular plot, and turns the grapes into the wine. Bouchard Père et Fils, the large négociant, owns 234.65 hectares of Burgundy, 175.37 of them *grands* or *premiers crus*, besides making much wine from grapes bought from outside. Yet the firm must blush as it reads its Parker. For each village he lists the most overrated producers. For village after village, the list includes Bouchard. Meanwhile, you get the impression that Philippe Leclerc or Hubert Lignier or Henri Jayer could make brilliant burgundy out of almost any grape in almost any year.

You can, of course, help yourself by choosing a merchant you trust. It is no good going to the big boys; the best burgundy is made in such minute quantities that it will not interest the large retailers. A small merchant, preferably a specialist, is indicated – Domaine Direct perhaps, or Haynes, Hanson and Clark. Unfortunately, burgundy's producers have the nap hand over the merchants. The man who fails to buy the bad vintage is unlikely to get the pick of the good which follows. So even the best of merchants is likely to carry less elevated wines. *Caveat emptor* rules except that if burgundy buyers truly *caveat*'ed, they would end up with empty cellars.

"I rejoice in Burgundy," wrote Evelyn Waugh, in *Brideshead Revisited*. "For centuries every language has been strained to define its beauty, and has produced only wild conceits or the stock epithets of the trade." All who worship this most tantalising and elusive of mistresses know what he means; and hope that this is the week that they find the bottle that really does exhaust the capabilities of mere words.

© *Times Newspapers Ltd* (6 July 1991)

———

Though personally no admirer of the French, of French manners and French morals, though I put no faith in French quality, abhor French centralisation, loathe from the very bottom of my heart French tyranny, and think that *French military glory – which is but a velvety euphemism for French brigandage and French invasion** – should be put down by the comity of nations and the strong will and strong arm of all mankind, yet I am of opinion that there is much in the French kitchen which might be advantageously transplanted and successfully imitated in this country.

KIRWAN, *Host and Guest or The Diner's Guide* (1864)

* Written when Napoleon III's military ambitions seemed to threaten Britain, and Tennyson, then Poet Laureate, was urging, 'Form, Form, Riflemen, Form' – C.R.

TWO CLASSIC CLARETS OF A CLASSIC YEAR

The year this book is published, 1992, is the year that the '89 clarets reach bottle, and it is heartening, after David Lipsey's gloom over the rarity of good burgundy and the virtual non-existence of great burgundies, to be reminded that there is always plenty of good claret and fine clarets still to come...

POMEROL: CHÂTEAU PÉTRUS AND THE '89

CYRIL RAY

The costliest and most sought-after of the great red wines of Bordeaux – I suppose of all France – is, as to its birthplace, the most unassuming.

The little byways that lead one into, and then crisscross the hamlet of Pomerol all carry signs directing you to this or that famous, not so famous or positively obscure château of the commune, not a one to Pétrus. (I need hardly add that the tiniest *gamin* or *gamine* in the street will direct you . . .)

"Intentional," said Frédéric Lospied, the public-relations man, and all that surprises you is that Pétrus goes so far as to have such an official, though young Monsieur Lospied could hardly convey information more modestly or with such delicate understatement. Good wine needs no push.

The château itself (so-called out of courtesy) though its name is elegantly lettered on a side-wall, and all is trim and well-ordered, is no more than a trim two-up, two-down house, with a reception room, a tasting room and cellars, and a couple of small private rooms above, in which no one lives.

In the reception room are an Edwardian painting and a 1950s

photograph of Madame Loubat, the widow who in effect 'created' Pétrus.

My wife and I were reminded of our first visit to this part of France, early in 1957, when we complimented Madame Daniel Querre of Monbousquet, in nearby Saint Emilion, on the glow and the smell of the wood fire over which our delicious lunch was being roasted. "Hélas!" she said, 'they are our vines . . .''

The cruel frost of 1956 – the greatest calamity to befall France's vineyards since the phylloxera plague swept across them almost a century earlier – had destroyed everyone's vines, and growers for miles around simply rooted them up and replanted, resigned to a wait of five years and more before they even saw fruit. Madame Querre told us how she had seen her husband weep for the first time in forty years of married life as he lamented, "The world will forget the name of Saint Emilion . . ."

Madame Loubat, whose husband had bought Pétrus in the 1920s, and who managed it after his death, thought otherwise. She had faith in the roots of her vines – for all I know she prayed over them – and, sure enough, they lived. When the vineyards of the region were reborn, hers were the only old vines.

All this was explained to us, in the presence of her portraits, by Christian Moueix, whose father, Jean-Pierre, now 74, bought half the Pétrus property after the widow's death in 1961 – the other half is owned by the elderly niece of Madame Loubat, who takes no active part in its management.

This is in 44-year-old Christian's hands, and although the Moueix family also owns about a dozen other properties in Pomerol and the neighbouring communes of Fronsac and Saint Emilion, Pétrus is the apple of the family's eye – the golden apple, indeed: we were at Pétrus the day we read in *The Times* that the New York 'futures' price for the 1989 Pétrus, still in cask in France, worked out at $250 (£130) a bottle. It will be much more when it reaches the shops, and who knows how much in the restaurants . . .

Christian Moueix shrugs shoulders rather than rubs hands over the price: costliness is a matter of course – not only must undeniable quality and consequent world-wide fame be taken into account but also rarity and the Pétrus *vignoble* is about 11 or 12 hectares in extent whereas the five famous 'first growths', Haut-Brion, Lafite, Latour,

Margaux and Mouton are approximately 44, 90, 60, 85 and 75, respectively.

In any case, producers of the finest clarets work on moderately modest profit margins – prices, and profits, multiply as their wines establish their true merit (as pronounced by such authoritative wine-journalists as the omniscient American, Robert Parker Jr) and as they pass through many hands.

Other great claret châteaux release each vintage to the wine-brokers in a succession of *tranches*, each dearer than the last: each Pétrus vintage, being so small, goes out in one go – after the others – in Britain, to the eminent independent house of Corney & Barrow, which lists it itself and distributes to others.

We tasted the 1989, straight from the wood, a legend before its lifetime has really begun (it would be the spring or even the winter of 1991 before bottling) and for its rich fullness and body recalled the Dutch writer Hubrecht Duijker's "food and drink combined" (and, irreverently, my wife's more vivid words on Guinness, "liquid steak").

Frédéric Lospied's view was that its depth and staying power would bring it to its peak for drinking in fifty years' time: Christian Moueix, casting a compassionate eye on my grey hairs, suggested a charitable twenty, and I salivated in anticipation – I shall be barely into my second century.

"The most colour and the most muscle" of the Bordeaux reds, again to quote its Dutch admirer, are attained by Pétrus, Christian Moueix says, partly because the average age of its vines is forty, (thanks to Madame Loubat) usually the peak of a vine's maturity, though some here are octogenarians. Other contributing benefits are the high proportion of clay in the soil, whereas all around is mostly gravelly or sandy; the retention of almost half the grape stalks in the pressing, to give backbone to the wine; and an especially long maturation.

Then, too, the rigorous 'crop-thinning' undertaken every June, when promising shoots are snipped from the vines *pour encourager les autres*, making them all the fewer and the richer. "Certain great vineyards in the Bordelais look for sixty hectolitres of wine from every hectare," they told me, "we aim at forty."

The average age of the vines is kept at a steady forty by clearing one hectare of the very oldest (vines are kept in 'blocks' according to age) every eight or ten years and then replanting: the new crop is vinified and kept separately until the vines are twelve years old – no wine in the Pétrus blend is younger than that.

When we visited Mouton the next day, Baronne Philippine de Rothschild marvelled when I told her that the splendid wine of Pétrus, which she admires enormously, was made of ninety-five per cent Merlot, five of Cabernet Franc (soon to dwindle to two.) Her father Baron Philippe, who had lived to see Mouton-Rothschild elevated, belatedly, to its rightful place among the *premiers crus*, thought Merlot a namby-pamby constituent in a classic claret: Mouton is made of ninety-five per cent Cabernet Sauvignon, five only of Merlot, for a little softness.

It is clear that many factors must be taken into account in explaining what makes Pétrus Pétrus, but Christian always goes back to first principles: "It's the clay," he says.

It was the first day of the 1990 vintage. Christian invited us to lunch with him and his 150 *vendangeurs* in the great bare *chai* behind the house – a lot of manpower for so small a vineyard, but these men, women and youngsters had been gathering grapes that morning at Château Magdelaine, the Moueix property in Saint Emilion. At Pétrus, picking is only in the afternoons, when there is no likelihood of finding morning dew still on the grape-skins.

It was a jolly gathering of old friends – staff and neighbours from Moueix vineyards all around. Our host was as much one of them as any, tucking as heartily into vegetable soup, pork chops – as many as you wanted – more being grilled al fresco as they were being eaten; petits pois with diced ham and little onions; hunks of cheese, good French bread and open litre-bottles of red wine being refilled as quickly as they were emptied.

The wine was from good vineyards in the Médoc, I was told, that had over-produced the amount permitted by law to an *appellation* – just as good, but sold cheap in quantity because the market price for a wine without a name is negligible. And Christian did as his *vendangeurs* all did: he *fait chabrot* – poured a little of it into the last of his soup, drinking the mixture from the plate, as we know we mustn't take tea from the saucer. It is the custom of the country.

I was reminded to ask the question I ask every grower of fine wine:

if he didn't drink his own wine in, say, a restaurant, what wine would he choose? And for the first time ever I heard a Bordelais actually *mention* burgundy – for a white wine he would always choose a burgundy, and he likes the red, too. Best of all, though – and, again, a surprise – for he went outside the region of which he is the exemplar, across the river to Médoc with a special mention of the good *bourgeois* growths there, with a Lanessan as his example, just as Eric de Rothschild of Lafite had once quoted Chasse-Spleen. Both are classic clarets that would be ranked among the *crus classés* in any new classifier.

Sotheby's Preview magazine (1990)

CHÂTEAU HAUT-BRION AND THE '89

ASA BRIGGS

Wine is made for drinking, yet a surprisingly large number of words have been devoted to it, particularly during the last 20 years. It is difficult to pick up any newspaper or periodical which does not include something about wine, not least in the business pages. Some of the writing is racy, some is heavy with jargon. In 1983 Ronald Searle, inventor of the term 'winespeak', noted how 'tortuous phrases' used to describe music became even more tortuous when they were applied to wine.

When I was invited to write a history of Haut-Brion, one of the world's great clarets, I was determined to write it in language that readers of all kinds can understand. It has been an exciting commission, for Haut-Brion has a history that stretches back to the 16th century and the wine is distinctive. It is produced on the outskirts of the city of Bordeaux on soil that could not take any other crop. The history of a great city and of a great vineyard are inextricably intertwined.

In 1855, when the wines of the Médoc were classified semi-officially for the first time, Haut-Brion was the only claret produced outside the limits of the Médoc which was described as a *premier cru*. Since then it has always been compared with Lafite, Latour and Margaux rather than with the other red wines of the Graves district where it is produced. This is a comparison of different kinds of excellence, and the grouping went back unofficially long before 1855.

Leaving comparisons aside, Haut-Brion is a *premier cru* in a very special sense. It was the first claret to be identified under its own name, before Lafite, Latour and Margaux – so-called 'new clarets' of the early 18th century – attracted foreign customers, particularly in England. The first time we hear of Haut-Brion in England is in the diary of Samuel Pepys in 1663. He had just visited the Royal Oak Tavern in Lombard Street, near the present Bank of England, and recorded happily in his diary that he had drunk there "a sort of French wine called Ho Bryan that hath a good and most particular taste that I never met with".

The other great 17th-century diarist, John Evelyn, also drew attention to the name, as did the American president Thomas Jefferson more than a century later. Jefferson, then American minister to *ancien-régime* France, ordered quantities of it, and had it shipped to him after he returned to the United States. It was appropriate that special bicentennial celebrations were held at Haut-Brion in 1987 to celebrate his visit there.

Subsequently there has been a strong American connection in the story of Haut-Brion. Not only has Haut-Brion commanded an enthusiastic market in New York, Dallas, San Francisco and many other places, but in 1935 the vineyard was bought by an American banker and businessman, Clarence Dillon. It has since been developed by his family, beginning with his son Douglas Dillon, who was American Ambassador to France in 1953. His grand-daughter Joan is now President of the company. In 1967 she married Prince Charles of Luxembourg and after his death Philippe de Novailles, Duc de Mouchy, a direct descendant of the 18th-century Duc de Mouchy, who was Governor of Gascony when Jefferson visited the vineyard.

Clarence Dillon lived to be 96, and the first owner of Haut-Brion, Jean de Pontac, who created the compact estate, lived to be 101. Born in 1488, four years before Columbus crossed the Atlantic, Jean did not marry until he was 37. Yet he was subsequently married three times, the last time at the age of 76, and he had a total of 15 children. His father had been a Bordeaux merchant, a 'new man', who acquired great wealth and established social status. Jean's instincts were entrepreneurial too, and when he started to build the first Château at Haut-Brion in 1549 it was a *château vinicole* (wine-producing), and not a fortified place designed for protection. Nonetheless, the times he lived in were times of trouble as well as of opportunity. He was engaged in a plot against Henri IV when he died in 1589.

If history can be as dramatic as this, why bother about legend? Yet there is one charming story concerning the origins of Haut-Brion that is still frequently believed. The Irish lawyer and wit Maurice Healy, nephew of Tim Healy, the first Governor General of the newly-formed Irish Free State (now the Republic of Ireland) invented an Irish connection with Haut-Brion that existed long before there was an American connection. He fancied that it could have been an Irish merchant, John O'Brien of Ross in County Cork – and this Irishman really existed – who gave his name to the 'Château d'Aubrion'. Haut-Brion was O'Brien! The tale appealed so much to Healy that he asked to be pardoned that a "theory" which he had first "formulated in jest" might not be far removed from the truth.

There had, indeed, been a real Irish connection with Bordeaux long before Haut-Brion. *The Book of Lismore* records that as early as the year AD 535 traders from southern Gaul sailed up the river Shannon and sold wine at Clonmacnoise. In the 18th century there was a further Irish connection, when the Irish (and the Scots) continued to drink claret in large quantities after the English had turned to port.

Even in the 20th century it is difficult to know where legend ends and history begins in the story of Clarence Dillon himself. It has been claimed that he bought Haut-Brion because of the weather. When he visited Bordeaux in 1935, looking for a vineyard to buy, it was not only Haut-Brion that was drawn to his attention. Another vineyard – and one that was to be much favoured by Americans – Cheval-Blanc, was thought to be on the market in 1934. So, too, was Château Ausone, associated, in legend at least, with the Roman beginnings of wine-making in the area.

It was a cold, foggy day when Dillon arrived in Bordeaux, and the 35 kilometres between the city and Cheval-Blanc seemed a long distance to go. On the way he had to buy a rug, and his driver got lost, and the very real charms of the St Emilion district were therefore kept from him. By contrast, Haut-Brion, "at the very gates of Bordeaux", as it had often been described, seemed just right.

The story might have been invented by Maurice Healy, who would doubtless have gone on to speculate about the effects of that particular fog not only on Haut-Brion, but on Cheval-Blanc and Ausone. In fact there was more to Dillon's choice than this. Haut-Brion was secured only after months of negotiation and advice.

The really significant wine-making developments at Haut-Brion had taken place not in the Middle Ages when English kings ruled in Bordeaux, nor in the years when Jean de Pontac consolidated the estate, but in the 17th and 18th centuries. The Pontac dynasty controlled Haut-Brion until 1694, giving their family name to the wine that they produced. It was sometimes known as Pontac or Pontack rather than Haut-Brion. The Pontac who did most to publicise it was François-Auguste, an extravagant and eccentric character, and a pioneer in wine marketing. After the Great Fire of London he opened a tavern called the Pontacks Head. The sign outside it is said to have portrayed the head of his father, the only French nobleman to be so identified in London, and inside the tavern the food was said to have been as good as the wine. Christopher Wren once dined there, as did Defoe and Swift. The members of the prestigious Royal Society, devoted to the cause of science, held their St Andrew's Day dinners there until 1746.

By then a technical as well as a marketing revolution had taken place in the Bordeaux vineyards. In the Middle Ages all the wines of Bordeaux were drunk in the year they were produced. They were *vins de l'année*. Little importance was attached to names. Any old wine that was left was either sold far more cheaply than the new or was turned into vinegar. Only in the 17th century did the arts and techniques of wine-making and of wine conservation develop to the stage where wines began to be known for their date and place of origin.

Another visitor to Haut-Brion around the time of the transformation was the philosopher John Locke, whose influence was to be great on both sides of the Atlantic. In 1678 he wrote: "Pontac, so much esteemed in England, grows on a rising country open to the west in a white sand mixed with a little gravel, which one would think would bear nothing. But there is such a particularity in the soil at M. de Pontac's that the merchants assured me that the wine growing in the very next vineyard, where there is only a ditch between, and the soil to appearance perfectly the same, was by no means so good."

It is not Nature, of course, that makes wine – although the graces of Nature are necessary to make outstanding wine – but people. There were great figures at Haut-Brion, managers as well as proprietors, who ensured that its quality was of the highest during the 18th and 19th centuries. After the Pontacs came the Fumels, another family that had moved into the aristocracy, and after the Fumels the Larrieux, a banking family who remained in possession until 1921. Joseph de Fumel was Mayor of Bordeaux at the beginning of the Revolution but he was later guillotined.

For a while the estate belonged to Talleyrand. There is no evidence, alas, that he ever visited Haut-Brion or that his great chef Carème ever served Haut-Brion at table. By then, however, there was a genuine French connection, and the last to be made. Napoleon might prefer Burgundy, but Haut-Brion was now as much appreciated in Paris as in London.

Great though the tradition in wine-making was during the late-17th and 18th centuries, there have been even greater changes in the late-20th century. Two managers at Haut-Brion, father and son, Georges and Jean-Bernard Delmas, have extended a great tradition. The latter, in particular, has brought to wine-making the skills of the scientist as well as the instinct and imagination of the artist. Controversially, he introduced stainless-steel vats in 1961 to enable more effective control of temperature during fermentation. In 1972 he introduced cloned vines into the Haut-Brion vineyard, recognising that it is not only the 'particularity of the soil' at Haut-Brion that counts but also the quality of the grapes. Jean Delmas has established himself as a leading figure in a business that is now managed better than ever.

Ultimately everything depends on the people who drink the wine. Haut-Brion is, in general, drier than the other *grands crus*. It is meant to be savoured, not relished. Its distinctive flavour builds up as it is tasted, just as wine itself builds up over the years. It is a wine that lasts until it acquires fullness of character. Some vintages have been called elegant, others complex, some flinty, some aromatic.

The recent history of the drinking of Haut-Brion brings in as many famous names as its more distant history. It was served in 1957 at a dinner given in the Elysée Palace for the Queen, two years later at a dinner for President Eisenhower, and 10 years after that at a dinner for President Nixon. At a dinner in 1973 Chou En-lai drank Haut-Brion, 1964. It now has many connoisseurs in Japan, and the Duc and Duchesse de Mouchy paid a visit there in 1989.

That year will stand out. It was a superb harvest, and when the century is over people will still be happily drinking Haut-Brion, 1989. It may indeed be the vintage by which the 20th-century Haut-Brion will be remembered.

Sotheby's *Preview* magazine (1991)

THOUGHTS ON VISITING ONE'S THOUSANDTH BOTTLING-PLANT

Bottles, bottles, everywhere, and not a drop to drink –
No plastic cork is drawn for us from sweet and sickly pink;
If only I had stayed at home –
Not bothered to come out –
I'd be in my pyjamas still,
And drinking bottled stout:

But I must do my duty, boys;
A wine-reporter, I,
And through the cellars I must go,
Although I am so dry.
The more I see of bottles, the less I get to drink:
A wine-reporter, boys, am I –
My God, it makes you think!

CYRIL RAY

PAUL BOCUSE:

"GOD, TOO, IS WELL-KNOWN ..."

MARCEL BERLINS

Paul Bocuse likes publicity, even if he's the last person in France to need it. The first cook-superstar since Escoffier, guru to a generation of *cuisiniers*, incontestably the Most Famous Chef in the World, he's recognized by Frenchmen more often than anyone except their presidents and Bardot. He's rich, lauded beyond superlatives, and full of awards and honours, including the highest, the *légion d'honneur* given him by Giscard d'Estaing (in return for which he created an exquisite black truffle soup, now available to mere customers at £27).

He did not need to celebrate his sixtieth birthday by posing nude for the pages of *Lui*, a kind of French *Playboy*, he did not need to do a television advertisement for a cooker, in which he's shown caressing and kissing it sensually, treating it as he would a woman. Undignified, vulgar, not serious, a personality cult, his detractors cry. *Mais oui*, he happily agrees – but what good publicity. Of course he's already famous, "but God, too, is well-known, yet the priests still ring the church bells every Sunday."

Bocuse is amiable, jovial and open about himself and all things culinary. He is more discreet on matters political – his friends and customers, from presidents downwards, cover the social and political spectrum, and they are too important to him to risk alienating by publicly trumpeting his no-doubt trenchant opinions. But he is not a modest man. Not many men – in any walk of life – would have arranged, even as a jest, a photographic version of Da Vinci's 'Last Supper', with himself in Christ's place and his chef disciples, all in correct uniform, gazing at him adoringly. He delights, too, in the little anecdotes about him – like how the morning high-speed TGV train from Paris to Lyons has been nicknamed 'le Bocuse', because so many customers travel on it to have lunch at his restaurant; and how former German president Heinemann is alleged to have said: "Lyons? Oh, yes. Isn't that a city near Bocuse's place?"

The gastronomic temple is a few miles out of Lyons, in the commune of Collonges-au-Mont-d'Or, although it's not necessary to know that because there are more signposts showing the way to Paul Bocuse than there are naming the village. Just in case, the restaurant proclaims his name in letters of a size usually reserved for large supermarkets. Bocuse was born in that very house. His father and grandfather were chefs, and the family's restaurant tradition in the village can be traced back for three centuries.

Inside, a huge portrait of the man, standing proudly in his kitchen, dominates the entrance to the tables. Smaller tributes – sculptures, paintings, photos – attack the visitor's every step. A large room is dedicated to the sale of Bocuse products – the predictable books (translated into more than a dozen languages), wines (he has his own vineyard) and gastronomic aids, but also a range of Bocuse trivia – model cars and cardboard pop-ups of the premises. His latest book, *My Classic Cuisine* (Pyramid Books) has just been published.

The gimmickry and occasional excesses are part of the most astute marketing operation in gastronomy. "Today, you have to know not just how to cook, but how to manage, and how to attract people to your establishment. If you are good in the kitchen but no good with figures and people, you must marry a wife who can run the business." He is as that remark suggests, no great champion of female chefs, and his 50-plus kitchen-staff and waiters are entirely male. His wife Raymonde is an elegant and charming hostess, but the role of women *chez* Bocuse is mostly limited to the social graces.

Bocuse's shrewd sense of marketing and the media produced publicity that went beyond his restaurant. All the top chefs benefited, as did Lyons's claim to be the gastronomic capital of France, and therefore the world. The breakthrough came with the 'invention' of *nouvelle cuisine*, with Bocuse more often than not described as its creator and father figure.

He's unhappy both with those labels and, no less, with what *nouvelle cuisine* has come to represent to many people. As originally conceived, *nouvelle cuisine* represented a return to fundamental principles of French cooking, a question of approach rather than individual dishes. "For me what it means is the use of the produce of the region – the best, which does not mean the most expensive; the produce of the season; the use of natural ingredients; and to cook them to bring out their smell and flavour, not to disguise them. But it's also a question of presentation, with nice tablecloths, and plates that are pleasing to the eye. I perhaps helped to make *nouvelle cuisine* popular, but for me the principles started with Fernand Point," he says. Homages to his mentor Point's restaurant in Vienne, where he served part of his apprenticeship during the Fifties are frequent in his conversation and on his menu. *Filet de sole Fernand Point aux nouilles fraîches* was voted by restaurant critic Henri Gault (co-founder of the *Gault Millau* guide) as the best single dish in any restaurant in France and "possibly the greatest dish in the world and in history".

Today his interests are world-wide. He has luxury delicatessens in a chain of Japanese department stores; a one-third share in a French restaurant in Florida's Disney World, which requires his presence there several weeks a year; and he has just masterminded a luxury restaurant staffed almost entirely by former Bocuse pupils, on board a Royal Viking cruise ship.

No one so successful can expect an easy ride from critics. The latest, most dramatic attack on his restaurant emerged from the 1989 edition of *Gault Millau*, the restaurant guide that many serious French food enthusiasts now consider more reliable, and certainly more lively, than the *Michelin*.

The accusation against Bocuse was that his frequent absences to deal with his other activities and interests had affected the gastronomic supremacy of his restaurant. To the accompaniment of national front-page headlines, *Gault Millau* demoted Bocuse from its maximum rating of four *toques* (chef's hats) to three, and reduced his marks from 19/20 to 18. That meant that the guide considered 21 French restaurants superior to Bocuse's, and more than 30 his equal, with the added insult that all the others had the compliment of their *toques* being coloured in red, to signify 'inventive cuisine'. Only Bocuse was outlined in black.

The guide's patronizing entry – written by Millau himself – praised the restaurant for its consistently high standards during Bocuse's absence; there was no risk of their slipping, it admitted.

"But if it remains sheltered from storms it no longer gives rise to thunderbolts." Excellent, in other words, but lacking flair, imagination, and the capacity to surprise.

'L'affaire Bocuse' quickly descended to the personal. If Millau's barbs were delivered in a tone of flowery pomposity, Bocuse's riposte was simple and direct. Millau, he said, knew little about food, and had to rely on the Jack Russell terrier that he insisted on bringing to the restaurants he visited. If the dog's tail wagged, the food was good.

But was he hurt by the demotion? "No, because I do not take Millau seriously. For me, the only serious guide is *Michelin*. Besides, Millau hasn't been here for three years. Don't you think if he was going to demote a chef he should come himself and not leave it to his inspectors? He is motivated by money and by publicity. I don't think that restaurant critics should be judges and participants as well. But Gault and Millau are consultants and they use their names to sell foodstuffs and all sorts of things. You don't see *Michelin* peas in the supermarkets."

He goes on in this vein, clearly enjoying himself, heaping libel on libel. "I am the only one who can hit back at these people. They have imposed rule by fear. The other chefs are scared to raise their voices. But me, I adore an argument." He adds, inevitably, that the whole affair has been good publicity. Far from business having suffered, "people are coming from everywhere to decide for themselves". In fairness, it has to be said that Millau has been far from routed; he has met Bocuse's frenetic insults with suave ripostes of equal malice and indiscretion.

Could there perhaps be just a tiny sliver of justification in the criticism that a man who is away for a total of several months a year cannot give his full attention to the cuisine of his restaurant? "When people ask me who does the cuisine when I'm away, I reply – exactly the same people as do it when I am here. After all, Fred Chandon doesn't personally put the champagne into bottles of Dom Pérignon. And, anyway, everyone knows that my chef-de-cuisine Roger Jaloux is one of the best chefs in France."

Bocuse, at 64, remains confident, unrepentant, combative, charming and conceited. He's enjoying life too much to think of slowing down, but occasional thoughts about the future are beginning to intrude. His daughter, in her early forties, is married and plays no part in the family business. His only son, Jerome, is 20, and studying the restaurant and hotel trade in Switzerland. So the succession of yet another Bocuse is assured? "Perhaps," he says. "Let's hope so."

SUNDAY LUNCH AT LE PALISSY

RUTH SILVESTRE

On Sundays, if we are not eating chez Bertrand or they with us, we like to go some ten kilometres away to the village of Lacapelle Biron. On the borders of Lot-et-Garonne, it was created almost by accident by a long forgotten Marquis of the nearby château of Biron. Suffering from both asthma and gout, this unfortunate nobleman could not bear the noisy market which was held each Monday beneath his walls. "Send them somewhere else," he wheezed and so, taking their name with them, the traders of Biron moved down the hill and across the fields to the ancient hamlet of Lacapelle. The two names joined together, the village flourished and Monday is still market day.

It is essential to book at the Restaurant Palissy which is named after Bernard Palissy, renaissance potter, scientist and philosopher. Born of humble parents in the next village of St Avit, he spent years researching his glazes, becoming so impoverished that he was reduced to burning his furniture and floorboards to fire his kiln. For Catherine de Medici he built a grotto in her Tuileries Gardens, decorating it with enamelled lizards, toads and serpents. He travelled widely and wrote on a wide range of subjects but always begged his students not to listen to those scientists who sat all day propounding theories. Always a craftsman he wrote "with all the theory in the world you can make nothing, not even a shoe. Practice must engender theory." He became a Huguenot and eventually Royal patronage could protect him no longer. He was imprisoned in the Bastille where, at the age of eighty-one, he died. There is a statue of him in Villeneuve-sur-Lot, a gentle, scholarly figure holding one of his famous dishes, a tiny creature curled up inside.

Outside the restaurant which bears his name the tables are always crowded with customers taking their aperitifs. "We have laid a hundred and seventy places today," announces M. Allo, the head waiter, as he greets us. Teeth flashing, M. Allo plays his role as though Feydeau himself had written it, glorying in every detail. Perhaps it is because he is really the local postman and only has two performances at the weekend. Otherwise he must tear across the countryside in his yellow van. Today all that is forgotten. Resplendent in a dazzling white, starched jacket, head to one side, he whirls and weaves between the tables at ever increasing speed. "*J'arrive. J'arrive!*" he calls, sweat already trickling down his florid face. He loves every moment.

The menu hardly ever varies but I suspect there would be an outcry if it did. This is what we come for, the *jambon du pays*, the *écrevisses*, the *ris de veau*. Restaurant Palissy is respected by local families and it is they who eat there in the winter when the tourists are far away. The dining room fills quickly. Many of the customers know each other and there is a lot of kissing. Most of the families are of three generations, all stylishly dressed, even though most of them will be at work in the fields tomorrow. Trays of melons, already on the table, perfume the room which reverberates with serious debate as menus are studied. The most expensive with seven courses will not cost more than twelve pounds and you can eat extremely well for seven. There is a choice for each course but no pressure to decide. Lunch will go on until four o'clock. Friends wave as the last stragglers take their places in the crowded room. *Bon appétit!*

Our soup is a tasty *consommé* in which float tiny beads of sago called, more poetically in France, *perles du Japon*. After the soup we sample the house wine, a *vin ordinaire* in name only, for the local Cahors is good. The melons are perfect; grown locally, they can be harvested at precisely the right moment. One of our party, not liking seafood, has chosen a cheaper menu. Her thin slices of home-cured ham hang over the edge of the plate. "Don't worry," we urge, "you have plenty of time." And we begin to demolish our mountain of langoustines, mussels, clams, winkles, prawns, shrimps and cockles in their shells.

M. Allo speeds past, balancing three trays piled with debris. He works twice as fast as the waitresses, all half his age, apart from his wife who is short, plump and calm, and smilingly approves his performance from across the room. "*Eh voilà!*" he beams and with a flourish presents the *écrevisses*, bright coral red, succulent and gleaming, sprinkled with chopped garlic and parsley and flambéed in Armagnac.

The first time we tasted *écrevisses* was chez Bertrand. Early one morning Grandpa had taken Mike and Matthew to his secret spot on a nearby stream. They had baited a line of square muslin nets with his special bait, chunks of pork fat dipped in Pernod. When the nets were slowly raised after a short wait the black shiny *écrevisses* were clinging to the underside, trying to reach the bait. "When I was a boy," grumbled the old man, "there were scores in this stream. Nowadays . . ." he shrugged, throwing his hands in the air.

In the event they caught a mere half dozen and the following day at Sunday lunch, after the first three courses, Claudette solemnly presented them in the centre of a large plate. "How are we going to divide them?" she asked. "I suppose those who caught them should have first choice." She put one on to each plate and then went back into the kitchen laughing, appearing again with a heaped bowl of *écrevisses* which she had generously bought at market.

Now, as then, we are surrounded by sounds of sucking and crunching and sighs of pleasure. Bread is dipped in the sauce and fingers finally licked before being almost reluctantly wiped on the scented tissues provided.

One of us had the *ris de veau*. "How were they?" we enquire. "Wonderful," she sighs, "have a taste." The sweetbreads are in a delicate sauce with olives and tiny mushrooms and they melt in the mouth. At every other table sampling of each others' dishes is going on. This is what Le Palissy is all about. Greasy-chinned faces beam at each other and M. Allo beams at everyone.

With our *rôti de veau* and *confit de poulet* we drink an older wine but still a Cahors. More sampling follows. We decide that the chicken has been preserved in goose fat, delicious! M. Allo brings a fresh green salad and then the cheese board which is small but interesting, a *bleu des Causses* from the stony hillside to the east, a fresh goat cheese and a Pyrenée.

Dessert is a choice of ice creams, chocolate, sorbet of lemon or blackcurrant, *vacherin* – vanilla with slices of prune inside, or a slice of *tourtière*. As he finally brings our coffee M. Allo is anxious to know if we have enjoyed our meal. We assure him it was wonderful. He beams. We have a favour to ask. May we take his photograph? His jaw drops. He stares at us blankly then rushes from the room. Have we offended him? He returns at a run frantically combing his hair, and poses. His great shoulders heave as he tries to suppress a sudden fit of giggles. In an effort to be serious he clasps his hands tightly. Click, it is done. He rushes off again to return moments later with a baked Alaska. It is a special treat for someone's birthday and with a flourish he lights the sparklers stuck in the top. As we leave Le Palissy customers still left are singing Happy Birthday, M. Allo as loudly as all the others.

Extract from *A House in the Sunflowers* (1991)

Housewarming at Zola's. Very tasty dinner, including some grouse whose scented flesh Daudet compared to an old courtesan's flesh marinated in a bidet.

The Goncourt Journals

CHAPON FIN AND CHAPEAU ROUGE

G. B. STERN

As we drove along between the crowding traffic of the quays at Bordeaux, we sank a little timidly into our seats, with the sensation that a fortnight in little friendly villages, and speeding along kindly roads, had robbed us of our city confidence. Bordeaux appeared overwhelming, and even the protection of Michelin seemed to be withdrawn from us, and only his cold curt directions remained. Altogether, we spent only three days in Bordeaux, and were glad to escape from it; a pitiful confession for four swaggering cosmopolitans, hitherto at home in London, Paris, Rome, Vienna, and Budapest, with a touch of patronage for those dwelling gently in rural pastures and unfrequented mountains.

In Bordeaux was the famous restaurant of the Chapon Fin, marked with four stars. The Chapeau Rouge, slightly less celebrated, had also four stars; and the Restaurant de la Presse had three. There are two other three-star restaurants in Bordeaux; and by way of a commentary on the excellence of all these, most of the hotels were marked in brackets: 'meublés'; that is to say, one could only sleep and not eat. Bien! In Bordeaux we did as the Bordelais. After our first night's surprise at discovering that ours was the only table occupied in the hotel restaurant, we lunched and dined out.

I am still mourning the wanton destruction of a bottle of 1914 Château Cos d'Estournel, which we drank that night; it was our first experience of how little the wine-waiters in that region appreciated the extreme delicacy of the treasures of which they are guardian. I know that a wine which behaves all the time like an invalid wife: "You mustn't shake me! You're tilting me an inch too much! My dear, *do* take care of my sediment . . . Just a wee bit too warm! Just a shade too cold!" does exact the utmost vigilance; but nevertheless

I can hardly bear to think of the glorious bouquet of the Cos d'Estournel, that familiar claret bouquet, which to me is like none other in the world . . . and then to remember its brilliance clouded thickly with sediment.

Especially as Humphrey said he did not care for it, with an inflexion of "I told you so"!

However, my spirits recovered in the night; and it was in a state of high expectation that we went to lunch at the Chapon Fin the next day. We were surprised, certainly, when 'The Good Capon', which from its name we had pictured as small and intimate, proved to be in reality a vast apartment, decorated as a grotto. With no wish to criticize, I wondered merely *why* a grotto? Had the man who originally conceived the idea, read T. E. Browne? Did he think it "a lovesome place, God wot; fringed plot, fern grot . . ."? It was exactly like a restaurant in fancy-dress: – Enter the Chapon Fin, dressed as a grotto!

Neither was the atmosphere intimate. The wine-waiter and the maître d'hôtel were just the merest shade aloof and preoccupied with their European reputation. I did not feel cherished at the Chapon Fin, but the cooking was undoubtedly divine. We ordered 'de la maison', whenever possible; feeling that here it would be worth while to follow the chef's own inspiration.

Hors d'oeuvres – a marvellous selection. Sole de la Maison – steamed, with mussels darkening the sauce. Pintade, again in a most glorious sauce, enshrining mushrooms and other happy items; and then Fraises de la Maison, delicious little wood-strawberries, snuggling beneath a smooth eiderdown of cream, faintly flavoured with almond.

We left the selection of our wines to the sommelier, and again I was slightly disappointed, though I believe he acted for the best. Perhaps he deemed it a pity to bring out his solemn great wines for what must have seemed to him like a light luncheon, lightly undertaken.

"You are eating guineafowl," he said. "With guineafowl, you must have a Pétrus."

Probably he was right. It was not for us to say; so we had a Château Pétrus, 1913, Pomerol, first growth; preceded, however, by a Chevalier, which is a delightful white wine to drink with fish. The mating of Pétrus with pintade may have been predestined by all the connoisseurs, but it just did not appeal to me; the Pétrus was too like Burgundy, and not enough like Bordeaux!

Humphrey and Rosemary liked it.

The Fine Champagne of 1869 could not have been bettered.

We dined at the Restaurant La Presse, a much homelier place, where we were waited upon by women, who all had the air of being daughters of the house. Oddly enough, this was the first restaurant in France where we were given fish-knives and forks. The meal was mostly memorable for a most beautiful Chablis 1899; a rather puzzling Chablis; for whereas from its fragrance and flavour it seemed undoubtedly genuine, its colour was a very deep gold; the true Chablis, so I had been warned over and over again, is always very pale and faintly greenish in hue.

The Chablis was followed by a Marquis de Terme 1911, a fourth growth of claret; I had sampled it a year before, from the cellars of Messrs. Steiner of San Remo; a fine and silky vintage of 1900. From the same cellar came a superlatively good Mouton Rothschild 1917; one of my sterner friends had told me that I was committing infanticide by daring to drink a 1917 Mouton Rothschild; and I suppose he was right, and that I ought to have waited another fifteen or twenty years, nursing my desire; nevertheless, those two clarets, the Marquis de Terme, and the eight-year-old Mouton Rothschild, were for some inexplicable reason better than every wine, except one, that I was to drink in Bordeaux itself, with the great Médoc country not five miles away, and Haut-Brion just beyond the city gates.

"Not very good, dear," said Rosemary, as she sipped the 1911 Marquis de Terme; and Humphrey said nothing at all.

I tried to console myself with quail, wrapped picturesquely in a strip of bacon-fat and a vine-leaf. I said that that dinner was memorable for the fish-knives and forks, and for the Chablis. I have forgotten one other outstanding incident, the collapse of Johnny, his one collapse during the whole tour, from too much food and drink. By an irony of chance, he had the day before invented and added to our perpetual vocabulary, the word 'glotto', signifying: 'gloriously glutted and blotto'. It seemed to us a good word; we hailed it with applause . . . And now none of us dared use it, even in a whisper!

On our last night in Bordeaux, we went to dine at the Chapeau Rouge. It was the most successful of our dinners. From the moment

we entered, we had a premonition that here all would be well. We
liked the plain room, with its Wedgwood panels. We liked the aura
of the maître d'hôtel, and decided at once that we preferred to be
waited on by men than by women: "There's always a touch of
'Come on, Father, dinner's ready!' about waitresses," remarked
Humphrey.

The maître d'hôtel gave us his full and interested attention. He
was a merry man, but not too merry. You must not be too merry
where food and drink are in question; – genial, but not jovial, should
be the waiter's motto. He only made one mistake, in suffering three
of us to order cold sole in aspic. It was an oppressively hot evening,
and our first impulse was to order almost everything iced; but he
should have warned us, with a touch of severity, that sole is a fish
that loses its flavour when cold. True, it was served with such a wonderful mayonnaise that this in itself was compensation; but Rosemary had decided independently on 'Cèpes Bordelais'; and they
smelt and looked so rich and delicious, and her expression on tasting
them was so ecstatic, that Humphrey and Johnny and I could not re-
frain from begging for alms from her plate, just enough to taste, for
she declared that never before had she eaten them so beautifully
cooked.

This is the recipe for Cèpes Bordelais, as spoken by the head-
waiter of the Chapeau Rouge, who had received it from the lips of
the chef of the Chapeau Rouge, in the manner that legends are
passed on, reverently – and often inaccurately, for I cannot vouch
that this is right: the heads of the cèpes are put into a casserole, with
olive oil, and cooked very slowly. In a separate pan have been cooking the stalks, chopped up. Take the stalks out of the pan, and cover
them with chopped parsley and garlic; and in a third pan bring some
more oil to the boil. Put the stalks, etc, into this pan, pour the whole
mixture over the heads, and serve.

Unfortunately, the maître d'hôtel turned round just at the
moment when the three little dabs of Cèpes Bordelais were being
shovelled on to the plates that had lately contained sole and mayonnaise. And, poor man, he nearly died of shock! Rushing forward,
but too late, he declared, sobbing, that he would have brought clean
plates, clean cutlery, more cèpes, *anything* . . . rather than that a
royal dish should meet with such indignity! He was, of course, quite

right. We apologized humbly, and did our best to recover a little esteem in his eyes. I think he recognized a glimmer of intelligence in our discussion over the wine-list; for he did not begin, in the way of most sommeliers when we asked them which was the gem of their cellars; for they usually took such a question as a confession of our own incompetence; and began to inform us indulgently that Bordeaux was a different wine from Burgundy; and that the quality of wine varied according to the date on the label . . .

("Tiens?" said Rosemary.)

Humphrey and Rosemary, when they had last travelled through France, had made one other discovery besides the great Romanée Conti at Mâcon. They had drunk Pouilly-sur-Loire in its native home, and recalled it as a delicious light white wine, very individual and fresh, with a flavour of flowers that is usually the property of Rhine wine alone. We drank Pouilly-sur-Loire now, and agreed with them in their liking for it, although they assured us it was not quite so good as doubtless we would have later, on our way to Beaune.

The big wine on which we banked our hopes was Château Ausone, that great first growth of Saint-Emilion. The date was 1906. The bottle was treated, we were profoundly thankful to see, in the manner of a cradled heir to a great house, where no more can be expected.

After all our disappointments, the first second of savouring and tasting was one of almost unbearable tension . . .

Then Johnny and I sighed in relief.

It was all right.

It was more than all right.

There were many beaux gestes on the part of Humphrey and Rosemary, which we as graciously received. Château Ausone had all the best characteristics which had won Bordeaux her crown and queenship. It was suave and melodious, with a marvellous bouquet. It lay softly on the tongue; and when it had slipped down the throat, it left behind it an echo and a dream.

There is always something hopelessly comic about duck; and I am afraid that when I begin raving about the duck which had been selected by me, and by me alone, at the Chapeau Rouge, I shall be rudely accused of anti-climax. But, you know, that duck! – you could almost drink it! Without any action of the jaw, it simply melted away in your mouth.

It was the tenderest duck I have ever eaten;
And they served it with petits pois,
And bacon,
And tiny frail onions.

Extract from *Bouquet* (1927)

CHEZ ROTHSCHILD

LADY MORGAN

It was on a lovely July evening, that we set forth by the *Champs Elysées*, on our dinner visit to the *château de Boulogne*, the beautiful villa of Monsieur de Rothschild;* and from the moment when the gates of the domain were thrown open for our admission, we found ourselves enclosed within a paradise, to which no one enjoyment, incidental to the first Eden, seemed wanting. Flowers of all regions, fruits of all climes, tropical birds, English verdure, French sunshine, living waters, sparkling on marble basins, and fresh

"As the dews which deck the morning flowers,
Or rain-drops twinkling in the sun-bright showers";

delicious music self-played, with ready, not obtrusive services noise-

* James Rothschild was to buy Château Lafite in 1868: his great-great grandson, Eric, now in control of Lafite, tells me that the villa described by Lady Morgan was situated in the Paris suburb of Boulogne (after which the Bois de Boulogne is named). It remained in the family but was neglected, and is now a ruin. – C.R.

lessly performed, were the preludes to admission into that salon, where we found the lady of the enchanted palace (not as my heated imagination expected, another Armida, but) in all the simple, honest charm of motherhood, surrounded by her lovely children.

A large society of distinguished persons of all nations, induced a very desultory and amusing conversation, during that *mauvais quarte d'heur* (generally so dull) which precedes the dinner. A few of the finest productions of the ancient and modern Flemish school adorned the apartments. The most superb toys that ever filled a round table, and scarce editions and ornamental works, occupied those who were indisposed to join in discussions carried on in all languages. Still, while talking to Gerard, and expecting Rossini, – the immortal Carème was not the less uppermost in my mind. Gerard was my old friend, Rossini my old acquaintance: but I was already acquainted with *their* works [...] But of the works of Carème I had yet no experience. I had yet to judge (in his own words) of those ameliorations in his art, produced by the "intellectual faculties of a renowned practitioner." I did not hear the announce of "*Madame est servie*" without emotion. We proceeded to the dining-room, not, as in England, by the printed orders of the red book, but by the law of the courtesy of nations, whose only distinctions are made in favour of the greatest strangers.

·   ·   ·

To do justice to the science and research of a dinner so served, would require a knowledge of the art equal to that which produced it. Its character, however, was, that it was in season, that it was up to its time, that it was in the spirit of the age, that there was no *perruque* in its composition, no trace of the wisdom of our ancestors in a single dish; no high-spiced sauces, no dark-brown gravies, no flavour of cayenne and allspice, no tincture of catsup and walnut pickle, no visible agency of those vulgar elements of cooking, of the good old times, fire and water. Distillations of the most delicate viands, extracted in "silver dews," with chemical precision, "on tepid clouds of rising steam," formed the *fond* of all. Every meat presented its own natural aroma; every vegetable its own shade of verdure. The *mayonese* was fried in ice, (like Ninon's description of Sevigné's heart,) and the tempered chill of the *plombière* (which held the place of the eternal *fondu* and *soufflets* of our English tables) anticipated the stronger shock, and broke it, of the exquisite *avalanche*, which, with the hue and odour of fresh gathered nectarines, satisfied every sense, and dissipated every coarser flavour.

With less genius than went to the composition of this dinner, men have written epic poems; and if crowns were distributed to cooks, as to actors, the wreath of Pasta or Sontag, (divine as *they* are) were never more fairly won than the laurel which should have graced the brow of Carême, for this specimen of the intellectual perfection of an art, the standard and gauge of modern civilization! On good cookery, depends good health; on good health, depends the permanence of a good organization; and on these, the whole excellence in the structure of human society. Cruelty, violence, and barbarism, were the characteristics of the men who fed upon the tough fibres of half-dressed oxen. Humanity, knowledge, and refinement belong to the living generation, whose tastes and temperance are regulated by the science of such philosophers as Carême, and such amphitryons as his employers.

As I was seated next to Monsieur Rothschild, I took occasion to insinuate, after the soup, (for who would utter a word before?) that I was not wholly unworthy of a place at a table served by Carême; that I was already acquainted with the merits of the man who had first declared against '*la cuisine epicée et aromatisée*;' and that though I had been accused of a tendency towards the *bonnet rouge* my true vocation was the *bonnet blanc*. I had, I said, long *goûté les ouvrages de Monsieur Carême* theoretically; and that now a practical acquaintance with them, filled me with a still higher admiration for his unrivalled talents.

"*Eh! bien*," said Monsieur Rothschild, laughing, "he, on his side, has also relished your works; and here is a proof of it."

I really blush, like Sterne's accusing spirit, as I give in the fact: but he pointed to a column of the most ingenious confectionary architecture, on which my name was inscribed in spun sugar. *My* name written in sugar! Ye Quarterlies and Blackwoods, and *tu Brute*, false and faithless Westminster! – ye who have never traced my proscribed name but in gall, – think of 'Lady Morgan' in sugar; and that, too, at a table surrounded by some of the great supporters of the holy alliance! – *je n'en revenais pas!*

All I could do, under my triumphant emotion, I did. I begged to be introduced to the celebrated and flattering artist, and promised, should I ever again trouble the public with my idleness, to devote a tributary page to his genius, and to my sense of his merits, literary and culinary. Carème was sent for after coffee, and was presented to me, in the vestibule of the château, by his master. He was a well-bred gentleman, perfectly free from pedantry, and, when we had mutually complimented each other on our respective works, he bowed himself out, and got into his carriage, which was waiting to take him to Paris.

Extract from France in 1824–30 (1831)

THE STAR-GAZER'S GUIDE

CHARLES HENNESSY

Although Cole Porter's exhaustive list of what constituted 'the tops' was necessarily circumscribed by the exigencies of his rhymes, it gives a fair idea of the kind of touchstones, or icons, by which we choose to measure our times. The Colosseum and the Louvre museum, the National Gallery and Garbo's salary, the *Mona Lisa* and the tower of Pisa, a Berlin ballad and a Waldorf salad (Porter lived in the Waldorf Towers, although not in his salad days), Mahatma Gandhi and Napoleon brandy, Mickey Mouse – Cellophane!

No doubt the completion of a couplet whose first line ends, "The Michelin guide to French restaurants and hotels", would present a challenge even to that whiz with words, but it would be surprising if this devout Francophile had not given the matter some thought, for in his Paris days the guide was already a quarter of a century old. (Porter's impact on the social life of the two most cosmopolitan of cities was brought home to me in the Fifties when, introduced to some worldly *rentier* as one who had recently arrived in Paris from New York, the man leaned urgently towards me and asked, "How is Cole?")

For me, the Big Red One is quite simply the greatest feat of collective authorship since the King James version of the Bible – a work whose details, alas, are rather less familiar to me. It is also, surely, the precursor of the symbolist movement: you do not so much read the Michelin as *decode* it. But it is more, much more, than that: it is the only one of my chosen travelling companions to have stayed the course, to have remained faithful through all our travels and travails, its pledge of fidelity renewed each year with the renewal of the year.

That indefatigable roadie, Richard Binns, the travel writer (and guide publisher), graciously concedes: "Since 1900 Michelin has been the guardian of hotel and restaurant standards in France." No small claim, that, from one who has followed the same trails. To Binns, the red Michelin guide to that country's incomparable good living is "a miracle of organisation; and in what it sets out to do it has no equal. Its superb maps are masterpieces and no other guide manages to pack so much into 1,200 pages." This, incidentally, from a map-freak whose guides are illustrated with his own work. The American government was no less appreciative. At the outbreak of war in 1939, it asked permission to reproduce the Michelin town plans for the use of the army.

"Living like God in France" is the German's happy phrase for the ultimate in pleasure, and the Michelin, France's greatest single contribution to the art of living well, is your surest guiding light to that desirable higher state.

That redoubtable epicurean Cyril Connolly, in *The Unquiet Grave*, knew the form: "Peeling off the kilometres to the tune of 'Blue Skies', sizzling down the long black liquid reaches of Nationale Sept, the plane trees going sha-sha-sha through the open window, the windscreen yellowing with crushed midges, she with the Michelin beside me, a handkerchief binding her hair . . ."

At the first Easter of the century André Michelin, foreseeing a brilliant future for the new-fangled car industry, brought out his first guide – a slim, red, 399-page volume, the size of a hymn book, bearing on its cover the device, "*Offert gracieusement aux chauffeurs*" (meaning gentlemen and lady motorists rather than their drivers). The preface unblushingly claimed: "This book, born with the century, will live as long."

This claim now seems a miracle of modesty: the Michelin, as Robert Frost said of five or six of his poems, will be hard to get rid of. Only war has kept it from publication, and by the first world conflict it was already a plump 600 pages and in a larger format.

Fired by its domestic success, the company went on to bring out foreign-language guides for Germany (1910) and, in the next year, to Great Britain and Ireland. By 1920 the French guide was up to 800 pages and was 8in by 4½in (it still is).

To the single star of 1926 were added two and three stars, all to provincial restaurants – Paris followed two years later. The stars, and the book, went out with the second world war and the progression began all over again: one star in 1947, two stars in 1949, three stars in 1951.

The masterstroke, though, was the introduction of the code. The first shy symbols were already there in the first edition. (There was a secondary advantage: the symbols cut out the gab. Who *cares* what a couple of upstart hacks like Gault and Millau have to say on a subject of such profound importance? Why, I have friends I would trust with my life that I would not trust with the choice of a restaurant.)

It has been calculated by whoever does that sort of thing that, but for the use of symbols, it would take six or seven volumes each of 1,000 pages for the French guide to cover all the classification of degree and quality of cuisine and service offered by the listed restaurants and hotels. So you have to crack the code; but never fear – an hour with the explanatory pages up front and the Michelin will be, well, an open book or, in Binns's words: "You'll find the guide ticks like a Swiss watch."

He gives an example. Look up Peillon in the French guide for 1991. The Michelin 'picture' is just over half-an-inch deep, yet is still a mine of information. You are told the village's postcode and département name, the numbers of two large-scale Michelin maps on which Peillon appears (and the section number on both maps), the relevant green (Michelin) guide, in which you will find more detailed topographical details, the number of inhabitants, the altitude, that both the village and the frescoes in its chapel are "interesting", the distance to Paris and six local towns and that Peillon is located on the Monaco local map (a 1990 innovation that shows you everything listed in the guide within 30 minutes' drive of the main centre).

The image-painting code continues; first informing you of the name of a pleasant, comfortable hotel with modern amenities and a very quiet setting, its telephone number, that it has an interesting view, a terrace (where meals are served), a garden and a tennis court, that bedrooms have direct-dial telephones; free car-parking is available and that dogs are not allowed in the 19 bedrooms. All closing dates are listed; and, finishing off, there are details of prices for meals (both during the week and on Sundays), a children's menu, bedrooms and breakfast.

All of this *multum in parvo* stuff would seem to predicate a vast, efficient and reliable infrastructure (and no small expenditure – a fact reflected perhaps in the company's current financial figures).

In France alone there are 15 full-time inspectors, stomping around the country for two weeks at a stretch, at the rate of two meals a day. A chef up for a star, or down for demotion, can reckon on up to a dozen visits, each a rigorous examination not only of cuisine but of welcome, quality of service, comfort, upkeep, quiet and pleasantness of location. Inspectors' files are supplemented by readers' reports – 100,000 a year for the French guide.

The inspectors travel incognito, until they have settled the bill – at which stage they ask the owner for a complete inspection. In their kindly way, they draw the attention of those concerned to certain failings to which they would do well to devote special care. (Chefs ignore the advice literally at their peril: one poor chap – at the Relais de Porquerolles in Paris, rather a favourite of mine – was deprived of his two stars in one go, lost heart and did himself in.)

For me, the Michelin has brought more joy than sorrow. It is amazing how many moments I associate with the Michelin or, more precisely and more sadly, that "she with the Michelin beside me". The warmly fresh baguette, the croissants, the Normandy butter, the bowls of *café-crème* on the balcony of the Normandy, looking down on the Parisians biffing a tennis ball and, beyond them, the far out, shrimp-rich sea; lunch of *ombre chevalier* at Le Père Bise in Talloires – three stars then, two now; the madcap dash from Paris to eat at L'Auberge de L'Ill at Illhausern in Alsace – *truffle sous le cendre* to kick off – the day the brothers got their third star; weekends at the Tortinière in Montbazon, with trout from the Loire in the orangerie; followed by dinner at Barrier in Tours – the *plateau de fromages de chèvre* with home-made walnut bread.

Ah, me: as the man almost said, *où sont les oeufs à la neige d'antan?*

The Times (June 1991)

. . . AS THE SPARKS FLY UPWARDS

I've tried, but it's always in vain,
Not to drink so much champagne,
But when I'm in trouble
I *do* need that bubble
– and it happens again and again . . .

CYRIL RAY

A RARE SPIRIT

BERNARD LEVIN

"No, I never go to cocktail parties," said Cyril Ray, "if you're my height, you walk about all evening talking to people's fly-buttons".

He *was* very short, but it was the crisp way he defined his problem that defined him, just as his nose, doubtless shaped in the womb, was perfectly formed to savour the scent of thousands of wines.

He was a truly lovable man, though he was also a strange basket of contradictions, foibles and obstinacies. I think that my first meeting with him was in the early Fifties, when he was still foaming at the mouth (again a most characteristic position) because of what *The Sunday Times* had done to him. And what *had* they done? Well, he had been their Moscow correspondent; one day, he understandably felt like getting away from the grim Soviet reality, and decided to go to the Moscow races. It was a beautiful summer's day, and he described the throng, the horses and the colours: "It was," he wrote, "like a perfect Dufy." Someone on the paper, no doubt fearing the ignorance of the readers, played safe, and after "a perfect Dufy", added ("a French painter").

The point of the story, however, is that the episode of the Dufy had taken place at least a year before; Cyril was one of those rare spirits who nurse grudges for a lifetime, *though only against follies, wickednesses and blunders, not human beings*. That meant wonderful hours in his company, hearing him fire off gorgeous libels in all directions, without the unease provoked by real misanthropists.

The contradictions, though. A socialist, he insisted on sending his son to Eton; a passionate freedom-lover, he swallowed naively much that he heard in Moscow; even when funds were low, he insisted on his weekly haircut; a prodigious pourer out of words, he

invariably insisted that he was the laziest man alive; a house too big
and expensive was matched to an implacable refusal to cut his coat
according to his cloth.

But all that was what we loved him for; and indeed, what Liz
loved him for, too, I'll be bound. His courage was remarkable, and it
was one of the few things that he was shy of discussing; it was
decades before I discovered that, as a war correspondent, he had
tossed a coin with one of his friendly rivals as to which would drop
at Arnhem and which at Nijmegen. Cyril picked Nijmegen; just as
well – if he had gone into the bag at Arnhem, the entire German
Army would have had a collective nervous breakdown, so madden-
ing a dance he would have led them as a prisoner-of-war.

It was his time on the *Spectator* that I think he felt most at home
and most content. Outwardly, people could think that he was an
irritable man, but that was only the veneer; he was wise enough to
confine himself to the things he could do, and to steer away from
those he couldn't – surely the clue to happiness.

I was yet another of the huge class who sat at his feet when wine
was being taught. I was an eager pupil, though he failed to make me
like port; but even the failure was characteristic – he coaxed and explained and offered, without the slightest hint of reproach. Cyril was
a man who relished life as he relished good wine and good food. The
grumbling was not serious, and I have no doubt that he woke every
morning eager for the day. I can see him now – plump, smiling, met-
iculous, ready to be fierce but happier being warm; a good friend,
and a loyal one.

A last reminiscence: the house in the country caught fire, and was
destroyed; no-one was hurt, and the fire spread so slowly that practically everything in it was rescued by Cyril and Liz, together with the
army of neighbours who turned out to help. But that was the problem, unforeseen. A few weeks after the catastrophe he rang me, in
great and mock distress. The problem was that when the helpful
neighbours promised to keep carefully the things they had saved,
each had taken a different item. Hear Cyril: "I don't mean to carp,"
he said. "They were all so helpful. But one of them took my suits,
another my shoes, another my underwear, another my shirts" – the
voice climbed – "I have to drive from house to house, and it takes me
three and a half hours to get dressed every bloody morning!"

TRAVELLERS'
TALES

IN PRAISE OF
OYSTERS

W. A. BENTLEY

My own love of oysters began when I was about twenty years old and living in New Zealand, where I was born. When I was still a child the colonists clung to their English habits of eating: they went so far as to cook turkey and plum-pudding for Christmas Day, although the mid-summer heat was so merciless that they had to doze under the trees when the incongruous feast was over. The New Zealanders neglected the beautiful food God had given them; the toheroas, which have since become a luxury, exported to America, lay neglected on the seashore, and the penguins' eggs were left on the rocks. Even oysters were so ill-treated that they were scooped out of their shells and sold in bottles.* But the Maoris, before the white men came, had been more delicate in their eating and they approached even their cannibal feasts with less savagery than we might suppose. Indeed it was claimed that when the missionaries came and Maoris cooked them, they could tell the difference between the denominations, preferring Church of England parsons as more salty and tasty, to Baptists and Methodists. This, of course, may be an exaggeration, but it is certain that the Maoris cooked their victims with quiet attention. There was an English master of a schooner trading between New South Wales and New Zealand in the 1840s. His name was Barnet Burns. He tired of the sea, went ashore and married the daughter of a Maori chief. He described a cannibal feast and the careful roasting of the woman who was to be the main dish:

---

* New Zealanders have since learned to respect and delight in their oysters. They enjoy both bed and rock oysters and, in 1940, the population of a million and three-quarters ate sixty-five million during the year.

She was ordered to prepare some potatoes for cooking with herself, and to gather green leaves for the oven. The savages made a large earth stove, laid the leaves on the hot stones, and tied both her legs together. When this was done, she took a friendly leave of two or three persons that she knew, and then threw herself down on the leaves ... They laid potatoes over her, and covered her with earth until she was cooked fit for eating.

This diversion is justified because it was through my interest in cannibalism that I came, by chance, to appreciate oysters eaten fresh from the rocks. Near Auckland, where I lived, was a delightful island named Kawau. Sir George Grey, one of our first governors, had retired there, with early Folios of Shakespeare and other treasures to console him for his isolation.

During his visit to Oceaná, in 1884–85, J. A. Froude went to stay with Sir George Grey at Kawau and he wrote of a cannibal 'banqueting hall' that he found there:

Here, at the beginning of this century, the Maori pirates of the island had held their festivals. To this place they had brought their prisoners; here they had slain them and hung their carcases on these branches to be cut up and sliced for spit or caldron . . . I could fancy that I saw the smoking fires, the hideous preparations, the dusky groups of savage warriors. I could hear the shrieks of the victims echoing through the hollows of the forest. We ourselves picked up relics of the old scenes: stone knives and chisels and axe-heads . . .

When I read this, sitting at a table in the Auckland library, I decided to go to Kawau Island and see what I could find. All was decay: the 'banqueting hall' was no more than a space of thirsty earth, between the trees, and Sir George Grey's early 'mansion' had become a stingy boarding-house. I shared my table with an Englishman – a stranger, who was silent, until the food was served. Tomato soup and steak-and-kidney pudding were followed by a steamed, lukewarm, spongy sweet, with a hideous pink sauce, the colour of carbolic. I refused it, with a smile. The stranger smiled also and said, "We seem to agree about that pudding". I told him that I had been to

the ruins of the cannibal banqueting hall and he said, "Well, I'd prefer a little cold missionary to that awful sweet". He applauded our
apples, our fish and our butter, and then described a plate of oysters
he had eaten on the day he arrived in New Zealand.

I answered, "But we can get oysters here."

He rested his hands on the table, looked ten years younger, and
said, "No! Can we?"

"Yes," I answered, "from the rocks. It is against the law, but that
doesn't matter."

"Do you mean to say that we can go out and actually pick fresh
oysters from the rocks? Could we have them for lunch tomorrow?"

I said, "Yes", and next day we set off, my companion carrying a
basket.

We found a little bay where the sand was clean and silver. The
beach was so hot that we could not bear to put our hands upon it.
The water was blue and smooth, with gulls swooping down and
piercing the surface with their beaks. The vast dome of the sky was
filled with silver light. At the end of the beach the rocks rose calmly
to the hills. We walked where there were pools with coloured sea-
weed, darting fishes and anemones in them. Wise old crabs scuttled
slowly over the shore.

We came upon a place where the oysters grew, packed together
close as grapes. My companion put the basket on the ground, and
took out two bottles, two glasses, two plates and two forks. I produced nothing but a chisel. I broke the oysters off, one by one,
choosing the big ones of tidy shape. The outsides of their shells were
still wet from the sea. We prised them open, carefully, to save the
liquor from spilling. Then we placed them, eighteen upon each plate.
My friend produced lemon and red pepper and I began to eat.

"Wait," he said. He opened the bottles, one of champagne and
one of stout, and filled the glasses. Thus I came to the pleasure of eating oysters with black velvet, sitting on a beach, with the blue ocean
stretched before me.

It is easy to imagine all kinds of delight into a past experience, but
I believe that my love of good food was awakened on that summer
day: the love of good food, laced with good conversation. My world
had been narrow up to then; what I ate had been no more than fuel
for my young body, and, although I was already devoted to my atlas,

because it was full of countries to which I might escape, I had never thought of the world, or of people, in terms of food, and wine. Now I know that they are the constant delight in travel, enduring long after landscapes have lost their charm.

I suppose that, apart from the pleasure of the oysters and the black velvet together, I was a little tipsy, because I remember lying back, looking at the clouds moving across the sky and thinking that they were like white meringue elephants on the march.

While I languished, in a nice state of well-fed levitation, my friend talked of food: of avocado pears, picked ripe from a tree in Africa, and dressed with nothing but oil and vinegar and a gesture of pepper and salt; of a baby lobster he had eaten – his first – when he was a student in Paris; of a journey in Russia when he ate fish stuffed with mushrooms. He talked of a world that was then beyond even my imagination.

In my haze I must have mentioned my ambition to write because as he gave me the last of the black velvet, my friend said, "I cannot write. I can only sketch, in a lazy way. If you mean what you say, some day, you must write in praise of oysters. They are the loveliest of all foods, raw or cooked."

Extract from *The Glorious Oyster* (1960)

We dined at Montreuil, much to our heart's content, on stinking mutton cutlets, addled eggs, and ditch water. Madame the hostess made her appearance in long lappets of bone lace and a sack of linsey-woolsey.

THOMAS GRAY: *Letters*

HOLLOW-HUNGRY

ERNEST HEMINGWAY

You got very hungry when you did not eat enough in Paris because all the bakery shops had such good things in the windows and people ate outside at tables on the sidewalk so that you saw and smelled the food. When you had given up journalism and were writing nothing that anyone in America would buy, explaining at home that you were lunching out with someone, the best place to go was the Luxembourg Gardens where you saw and smelled nothing to eat all the way from the Place de l'Observatoire to the rue de Vaugirard. There you could always go into the Luxembourg Museum and all the paintings were sharpened and clearer and more beautiful if you were belly-empty, hollow-hungry. I learned to understand Cézanne much better and to see truly how he made landscapes when I was hungry. I used to wonder if he were hungry too when he painted; but I thought possibly it was only that he had forgotten to eat. It was one of those unsound but illuminating thoughts you have when you have been sleepless or hungry. Later I thought Cézanne was probably hungry in a different way.

After you came out of the Luxembourg you could walk down the narrow rue Férou to the Place St-Sulpice and there were still no restaurants, only the quiet square with its benches and trees. There was a fountain with lions, and pigeons walked on the pavement and perched on the statues of the bishops. There was the church and there were shops selling religious objects and vestments on the north side of the square.

From this square you could not go farther towards the river without passing shops selling fruits, vegetables, wines, or bakery and pastry shops. But by choosing your way carefully you could work on your right around the grey and white stone church and reach the rue de l'Odéon and turn up to your right towards Sylvia Beach's bookshop and on your way you did not pass too many places where things to eat were sold. The rue de l'Odéon was bare of eating places until you reached the square, where there were three restaurants.

By the time you reached 12 rue de l'Odéon your hunger was contained but all of your perceptions were heightened again. The photographs looked different and you saw books that you had never seen before.

"You're too thin, Hemingway," Sylvia would say. "Are you eating enough?"

"Sure."

"What did you eat for lunch?"

My stomach would turn over and I would say, "I'm going home for lunch now."

"At three o'clock?"

"I didn't know it was that late." [...]

"Get home now before it's too late for lunch."

"They'll save it."

"Don't eat cold food either. Eat a good hot lunch."

"Did I have any mail?"

"I don't think so. But let me look."

She looked and found a note and looked up happily and then opened a closed door in her desk.

"This came while I was out," she said. It was a letter and it felt as though it had money in it. "Wedderkop," Sylvia said.

"It must be from *Der Querschnitt*. Did you see Wedderkop?"

"No. But he was here with George. He'll see you. Don't worry. Perhaps he wanted to pay you first."

"It's six hundred francs. He says there will be more."

"I'm awfully glad you reminded me to look. Dear Mr Awfully Nice."

"It's damned funny that Germany is the only place I can sell anything. To him and the *Frankfurter Zeitung*."

.   .   .

Outside on the rue de l'Odéon I was disgusted with myself for having complained about things. I was doing what I did of my own free will and I was doing it stupidly. I should have bought a large piece of bread and eaten it instead of skipping a meal. I could taste the brown lovely crust. But it is dry in your mouth without something to drink. You God-damn complainer. You dirty phony saint and martyr, I said to myself. You quit journalism of your own accord. You have credit and Sylvia would have loaned you money. She has, plenty of times. Sure. And then the next thing you would be compromising on something else. Hunger is healthy and the pictures do look better when you are hungry. Eating is wonderful too and do you know where you are going to eat right now?

Lipp's is where you are going to eat, and drink too.

It was a quick walk to Lipp's and every place I passed that my stomach noticed as quickly as my eyes or my nose made the walk an added pleasure. There were few people in the *brasserie* and when I sat down on the bench against the wall with the mirror in back and a table in front and the waiter asked if I wanted beer I asked for a *distingué*, the big glass mug that held a litre, and for potato salad.

The beer was very cold and wonderful to drink. The *pommes à l'huile* were firm and marinated and the olive oil delicious. I ground black pepper over the potatoes and moistened the bread in the olive oil. After the first heavy draught of beer I drank and ate very slowly. When the *pommes à l'huile* were gone I ordered another serving and a *cervelas*. This was a sausage like a heavy, wide frankfurter split in two and covered with a special mustard sauce.

I mopped up all the oil and all of the sauce with bread and drank the beer slowly until it began to lose its coldness and then I finished it and ordered a *demi* and watched it drawn. It seemed colder than the *distingué* and I drank half of it. [...]

I sat in a corner with the afternoon light coming in over my shoulder and wrote in the notebook. The waiter bought me a *café crème* and I drank half of it when it cooled and left it on the table while I wrote. [...]

There were days ahead to be doing that each day. No other thing mattered. In my pocket was the money from Germany so there was no problem. When that was gone some other money would come in.

All I must do now was stay sound and good in my head until morning when I would start to work again.

Extract from *A Moveable Feast* (1964)

A VISIT TO
MOUTON-ROTHSCHILD

CYRIL RAY

In the last article he wrote – for Sotheby's Preview *magazine – Cyril Ray interviewed the châtelaine of Mouton-Rothschild and found her 'one of a kind'.*

Château Mouton-Rothschild's Museum of Wine in Art receives a two-star rating in the *Guide Michelin* – *"mérite un détour"*. When I first stayed at Mouton, nearly twenty years ago, Baron Philippe said of it, "Mouton is a ship laden with cargo: a museum is a voyage", thus providing me with the closing words of the book I was writing on the château and its treasures. So I was delighted when, recently, again at Mouton, I learned from Baroness Philippine de Rothschild – in charge since her father's death in 1988 – of her plans for the ship and its voyage.

The Baroness is well aware that the captain's first duty is to the wine, but, given the soil, the climate, the classic vines and the vast amount of knowledge, experience – and, indeed, of pride – embodied in those who grow, make and mature life-enhancing Mouton-Rothschild, the ship is almost on the nautical equivalent of automatic pilot.

The Baroness fosters the pride of her people and promotes the prestige of her wine, at home and abroad, and still finds time to spare for Mouton's other treasures. She talked of them over dinner, at which we drank, first, Robert Mondavi's 1985 Chardonnay, collateral descendant of the Napa Valley Chardonnay that wiped the eye of the white burgundy producers in Steven Spurrier's celebrated comparative tasting in Paris on 24 May 1976.

It was this event that put California wines so firmly on the map that their growers became able to sell them to those on the other side of the Rockies who had gone on spurning 'domestic' wines long after we had shown here that we knew quality when we tasted it.

On this occasion the white wine was a reminder of the red Cabernet Sauvignon – product of the Mondavi–Mouton joint venture,
cemented in 1980, with the object, as I wrote after talking to Bob
Mondavi in the Napa Valley and to Philippe de Rothschild at Mouton, "of producing a wine with a personality of its own, neither
Mondavi nor Mouton . . . made jointly by two of the most highly
skilled, experienced and dedicated wine-making teams in the world
of wine". It was christened Opus One and Baroness Philippine de
Rothschild is as assiduous in promoting it as she is in presiding over
the production and distribution of Mouton: jointly-owned
vineyards in the Napa Valley have been extended; production has
increased (there is enough now for export); and at the time of writing there are a very few dozen of the 1982 and the 1983 spread
among some Majestic Warehouses in England. At a blind tasting
organised by New York's leading restaurants of outstanding 1982
Cabernet Sauvignons from California and Bordeaux, Opus One was
the top from California, beaten only by three first-growth clarets:
Cheval Blanc; its own cousin, Mouton; and Margaux; along with
another *cru classé* Lynch-Bages – very like Mouton in style. In
England the Cheval Blanc is £80 a bottle, the Opus One £35.

With roast duck came the 1934 Mouton, a fine if not a great year
for Mouton ('*Bonne Année*' in the Château's records) and *vrai
Mouton* in character, but "showing its age a little", said the Baroness of its finish, which is more than anyone could say of the
Baroness, whose birth-year it also was; she could have been of the
1949 vintage ('*très Bonne Année*') to look at, with quite a family
resemblance to her father, and the same heartfelt dedication to
Mouton and all that pertains thereto, expressed with even more
animation in a face more mobile – one might even say quirky – as
well as unquestionably attractive; as is to be expected in one who, as
Philippine Pascal, was a distinguished figure on the Paris stage (and
who married, in 1961, Jacques Sereys of the Comédie Française).

She was quick to pick up that phrase of her father's when I quoted
it to her – likening Mouton to a ship and its museum as a voyage: she
has no intention of its being put into dry dock. She is properly proud
of it, but feels strongly that it should now bring in works of art of the
nineteenth and twentieth centuries – it currently includes little later

than the eighteenth – perhaps in a specially designed extension.

The Baroness has the taste and the judgment to do it and, the theatre still in her blood, to make Mouton a centre, too, for the performing arts – a theatre workshop, perhaps; a concert hall? She admires what Bob and Margrit have done in the way of exhibitions and performances at the Mondavi Winery, so imaginatively designed by the Californian Cliff May – stopping short, perhaps, of its annual jazz festival.

A big task on which she is determined, one reminiscent of Philippe's long and eventually victorious struggle to have Mouton-Rothschild elevated into the first growths, is to rebuild the prestige of Mouton Cadet. Not the sales – at 17 million bottles a year few brand-name wines, if any, outsell it – but to restore its dignity, so to speak.

By a happy coincidence, the Baroness and Mouton Cadet share a birthday. The years 1931, 1932 and 1933 were disastrous at Mouton, as at the other great châteaux of the Médoc: in the Mouton records, *mauvaise*, *médiocre* and *mauvaise*, respectively: two marks each out of 20 in the *note qualitative*. The 1934 scored 14.

Philippe de Rothschild would not sell any of his 1930, 1931 or 1932 as Mouton-Rothschild, but this is not to say that they were not worth saving: in 1934 a blend was made of the best of them and sold as 'Mouton Cadet' under the *appellation* 'Bordeaux', not even as 'Pauillac' or 'Médoc', for some wines were brought from St-Emilion or Pomerol to give body. It was well made; there was a shortage of good clarets after the three lean years: here was a respectable Bordeaux, blended and matured to be ready to drink while claret-lovers waited for their splendid 1928s and 1929s to grow up.

It was a Good Thing welcomed as such by those who appreciate Good Things among clarets but, as Falstaff observed, "it was always yet the trick of our English nation, if they have a good thing to make it too common".

What had at first pleased the cognoscenti of claret became so widely available that, as older wines became ready to drink and new vintages became available for laying down, it became chic to dismiss it as simply another mass-market brand-name.

It is significant that there is no mention of Mouton Cadet in Clive Coates' magisterial and otherwise exhaustive *The Wines of France* (1990). Surely a vintage-dated wine with a Bordeaux *appellation*,

made from the classic grapes of the region by the people who make
Mouton, or people trained by them, deserved better than to be
elbowed out of the section on the region by its mere two *vins de pays*,
one of which the author says he had never heard, the other "shallow
and acid . . . thin and rustic"?

Fortunately for those who are glad to have what Edmund Pen-
ning-Rowsell has condescended to call a 'reliable' claret, at a modest
price, the 1986 and 1987 are available as I write at such chains as
Victoria Wine and Oddbins at about £5.50. Perhaps they would be
more highly regarded by some if they were twice the price and less
easily available. (Vintage dates for Mouton Cadet are an indication
of age – I should give each a year or two more cellar-age, as I would
non-vintage champagne. The years as such are not otherwise
relevant: the wine is blended from different parts of the Bordelais in
different proportions to maintain a consistent style.)

Baroness Philippine de Rothschild has a job on here, and I hope
she will be as successful as her father was in his fight for Mouton's
rightful status. Meanwhile, it is a measure of the lady's breadth of
mind that when I asked what wines she would ask for if away from
her own, she said, "Oh, I like to know what other countries are
doing – Chile or New Zealand or Bulgaria."

In thirty-odd years of writing about wine I had never known a
French wine-grower look outside France – indeed, except for Christian Moueix of Pétrus opting for white burgundy, none outside his
own region. But then the Baroness is one of a kind. I don't know the
French for 'chip off the old block'.

THE MASTER'S BROTHER:
A TALL STORY

WYNFORD VAUGHAN-THOMAS

It seems a long time ago – over forty years back as I write this – but I still have vivid memories of the first bottle of wine I drank after I had landed with the French army in the south of France on 15 August 1944. I wish I could claim that it was a noble bottle, worthy of the occasion. It was nothing of the sort. It was a strong Provençal wine, of nondescript origin, but presented to me free by a café owner in a little village behind St Tropez, who had been carried away by the excitement of finding himself suddenly liberated.

Now, even the French experts don't glow with enthusiasm when they discuss the wines of Provence and Languedoc. "*Les vins du Midi*," they pontificate, "*on les avale; on ne les déguste pas.*" In other words, you don't savour the wines of the south of France, you just gulp 'em down. But the pundits who advise you on how to judge wine always leave out one important element in your enjoyment of a bottle – the time and the place where you drink it.

I learnt that lesson in the days before the war, when it was still possible to get into a car and drive across the Continent as far as the Black Sea if you wanted to. A friend and I set off on this delightful journey and eventually drove into Budapest – long before the Iron Curtain was even dreamt of. We found ourselves entertaining two delightful young Hungarian ladies in a café on Margaret Island and drinking wines from Lake Balaton. I have never drunk any Hungarian wines since, but they live in my memory as nectar for the gods.

A total illusion of course, but it was a starlit night, there was a gypsy violinist plucking at our heartstrings and a cimbalom player tinkling up and down the scales. This was the Hungary of popular romance with not a detail missing. And I wasn't surprised when, later at dawn, my friend found himself in the flat with one of the young ladies who had obviously granted him her supreme favours.

He was no Adonis and could not help asking, as he gave her his grateful thanks, "How can I express my gratitude? Why have you been so kind to me?" She smiled up at him, "But it was to improve my English."

The bottle of Provençal wine had the same romantic aura to me as the Balaton wines I had drunk in Budapest. Again the quality of the wines did not matter. The time and the place were right. After all, we had just come ashore in the easiest landing of the whole war. We had put down a tremendous barrage and dashed for the shore, expecting to be mown down by machine-guns. Not a single bullet whistled past us: the Germans had tactfully pulled out a few hours before, and in their place an immaculately dressed Frenchman advanced out of the dust of war. He carried a tray with a magnum of champagne and ten glasses. The war in our sector stopped immediately. "*Soyez les bienvenus*," he beamed in welcome. Then he added, "Yes, welcome, gentlemen, welcome; but if I may venture a little criticism, you *are* four years late!"

Four years late or not – it didn't matter. We drove rapidly inland. On that August day, the whole of Provence seemed to be offering itself to us free.

It was at this point that I met the only Allied soldier who didn't seem to know what on earth was happening, the only totally bewildered liberator. As I drove my jeep past the long lines of advancing infantry and the little knots of country folk cheering and waving Tricolours at every crossroad, another jeep drew up alongside me and an unmistakably British voice shouted, "See you are flying the Union Jack. Mind if I join you?" It was thus that I met the Colonel – the most improbable of all military figures to be found attached to a fast-moving modern army ... Apparently he had been landed to "liaise" with the French in some mysterious capacity and was the supreme example of the gift the British army has for posting extremely square officers in extremely round positions. "Don't speak the lingo, old boy," he confided to me: "Learnt a little Pashtu on the Frontier, but it doesn't seem to go down well here." I invited him to join me in the nearby café, where the proprietor had spotted our British uniforms and was already preparing a meal for the brave liberators. It would be free. How sadly I feel the contrast these days when I go to France, where the restaurateurs cannot wait to slap the

bill before you when they find out that you are English. All old liberators will know the feeling. But on that mellow afternoon in August
1944, bills were an irrelevance. With that bottle of Provençal wine
before us, I could contemplate my new acquaintance with the interest of a biologist contemplating a new specimen. We shall not see
his like again. The Raj has disappeared into the mists of history, and
by no stretch of the imagination can I see him fitting into the stream-
lined, professional British army of today. He admitted that he had
arrived at the south of France landing by the old-fashioned way of
"knowing a pal in the War House who'd served with me in India, old
boy. Got back home in '39 when this little bit of bother blew up.
Had to get into it, of course."

At that moment the proprietor proudly laid the main course
before us – a rich dish which I did not recognise but which tasted delicious. We tucked in with gusto, and at last sat back happily to sample the cognac. Our host enquired anxiously if we had enjoyed our
meal. We assented vigorously and the proprietor beamed. *"Ah, je
vois, messieurs, que vous êtes les hippophages?"* "What does he
say?" asked the Colonel. I had to take the risk of translating. 'He
asks if we are keen horse-meat eaters." "Good God," spluttered the
Colonel, "I've been eating horse; and my brother's an MFH!"

Extract from *How I Liberated Burgundy and Other Vinous Tales* (1985)

En juin et janvier, la *romaria* de São Gonçalo, patron de la ville et
protecteur des mariages, attite à Amarante une affluence considér-
able. A cette occasion on fabrique des gâteaux en forme de phallus
que les jeunes hommes et les jeunes femmes ne se gènent pas de se
demander et de s'offrir mutuellement.

Guide Bleu: Portugal

SAMPHIRE GATHERING

DEIRDRE McQUILLAN

Stooping under the wide East Anglian sky are the samphire gatherers. Backs bent, bums up, disappearing into a land-into-seascape where complete absorption is always a possibility. Steep banks divide fields from the marsh and 24ft tides; houseboats used by duck hunters, now stranded on bright marsh grass, are firmly moored against the sea's return.

As soon as we climb the bank Paul Grief spots his competitors. "I think that's my cousins over there," he says, pointing at two dots I can barely see towards the horizon. "Everyone's here today," (we had already seen half-a-dozen others out gathering) "which is just daft because the samphire isn't big enough yet. Someone starts picking early and my buyers get on to me saying why haven't I got any to them yet, giving me a hard time. So the season gets earlier and I have to work twice as hard to get a bagful."

Samphire gatherers are rather secretive about where they go – another changed her mind about taking me out – because there are rarely any rights to this sort of fossicking. Landowners, such as the local duck shooting club or the Army, may restrict access to the shore, but the coast along which this aromatic, fleshy plant grows belongs to the Crown. Beaches are treated as public property, and so is samphire.

We are at one of Mr Grief's more obvious sites, a stretch of the Wash at Wolferton, quite close to King's Lynn where he lives, but he is not too pleased either with the other collectors or with the state of the samphire.

"There is not enough of it, to start with. The banks of the gullies and those mud-flats should be covered with a fine carpet of the stuff by now, but they are quite bare." We look at the bald, slimy banks and the hexagonal pavement of mud. The first slim green shoots are dismissed as "a thousand and one, that's what I call it. Those single stems are hardly worth picking." Eventually a specimen suits. It is thick and branched, like a cartoon cactus. But it is too small.

"It should be six inches or so for easy picking – that way the bag fills up quickly. A bit more time would make all the difference. Traditionally, samphire should start around midsummer's day. It will run all the way through until August but people will have had enough of it by then."

He sounds quite happy with these hardships. "It is just like strawberries, there's a great fuss to get the early ones out, then they go off the idea."

In June though, more and more people have gone on to samphire. The demand in East Anglia has risen steadily since Paul Grief began gathering 10 years ago. Here it is often eaten at the beginning of a meal by itself, quickly cooked and mixed with a little vinegar. Fishmongers and restaurants around the country snap up any that is offered outside the area, usually to be eaten with fish. East Anglian prices are 70p a pound but in London prices – nearer £1.25 – make its nickname, the poor man's asparagus, rather out of date. Marsh samphire (*Salicornia europaea*) tastes like particularly succulent, salty green beans. Any similarity of flavour to asparagus escapes me, although both are green, straight and seasonal.

Samphire, pronounced "samfer" where it grows, is a salt-tolerant member of the plant group that includes beet, spinach and chard. It was once burned to produce alkali for soap and glass making, which gives it the alias glasswort. As well as parts of the Norfolk and Suffolk coast, it is found in Wales and northern France.

The name really belongs to *Crithmum maritimum*, the rock plant that was more appropriately called St Peter's or Saint Pierre's. Rock samphire has fat leaves and a strong aroma. It used to be gathered for pickling along the south coast. Marsh samphire is also pickled at the end of its season when the seeds start to appear.

The best samphire we can find is at the point where the marsh vegetation peters out into bird-tracked mud. Little pools, left by the last big tide, hold some of the best branches because they are sheltered from the wind.

Paul Grief shows me how to pull the plant out with a twist, so that most of the mud stays behind and only the white roots come up. Muck gets under my nails, but I am quite impressed with our bucket of gleaming stems until I am told it is barely three quid's worth of work.

Mr Grief reckons the grass is choking off the samphire at this particular marsh, and perhaps that over-gathering has not left enough mature plants to spread their fine white dust of seed and re-fertilise the area. "The old boys will tell you about coming back with 20 sacks in a day, no trouble. Now 10 is hard work."

Having passed up the more secure option of becoming a docker in order to fish, Paul Grief picks samphire between trips. He uses his small boat to dredge for shellfish and started samphiring during a bad spell in cockles (there is currently such a bad spell of cockles in the Wash that fishing is banned).

His knowledge of the area, which began as a boy being chased off Sandringham estate by the gamekeeper, takes him to parts of the coast accessible only by foot or boat. Sometimes he pushes the full sacks back slung across an old bike. Once home the samphire is washed clean of mud, air dried, then put in clean string bags to go to shops and wholesalers.

Collecting the coastal plant fits well with his mussel gathering but it is the mussels, which mostly go to France, that earn him a living. "The samphire is just something to keep busy with, it would never make you rich. I'd be better off picking strawberries," he shouts contentedly, against the din of gulls and skylarks.

How to cook samphire: Wash and trim off the white roots. Cook for 3–4 minutes in fast boiling water, drain and eat dripping with fresh butter. The bright colour and firm texture are good with plainly cooked fish, and it adds a pleasant sea flavour to plain-tasting fish.

Independent (16 June 1990)

GREAT TASTINGS

MICHAEL BROADBENT MW

My move to Christie's in 1966 was well timed. The wine market was fragmented and, in starting a brand new wine department, the company immediately tapped a rich vein, unearthing – almost literally – cellars of old wine to satisfy an increasingly international demand. 'Collectors', as they are called somewhat pejoratively by those who are not of their bent, soon started acquiring great classics hitherto denied them and about which they had only read. At first these classic wines were consumed at wine-orientated dinners; soon after, when a sufficiently large range of châteaux and vintages had been accumulated, comparative tastings were organized.

Apart from trade tastings of young vintages, the concept of serious, often spectacular tastings of great wines and vintages organized by amateurs did not really exist before the mid-1970s. The first really memorable 'vertical' tasting (comparing several vintages of the same wine) was of 47 vintages of Château Latour. Organized by Marvin Overton, a neurosurgeon, at his home in Fort Worth, Texas, it was a black tie evening event. Representing France, and Latour, was Henri Martin, a director of the château, and at the other end of the specially-made vast oval table, behind the British flag, was myself, 'moderator' and commentator.

This was in May 1976. Three years later Dr Overton hosted a 'modest' tasting of Château Lafite, just 30 vintages, but chosen to represent every decade from the 1960s back to the 1790s. This time Baron Elie de Rothschild, who had brought from the château some of the oldest wines, sat opposite, and Hugh Johnson and Cyril Ray supplemented the English contingent. The rest of Dr Overton's guests included wine producers Robert Mondavi and John Parducci; the doyen of Napa Valley winemakers, André Tschelistcheff, and a mixture of American wine merchants and amateur enthusiasts. As at the Latour tasting, the wines were served in descending vintage order, that is to say starting with the youngest and ending with the oldest. This has a certain logic, but one tends to spend time and energy on the young and relatively tannic wines so that, nearing midnight, when the 'golden oldies' appear, one's taste-buds are flagging. Nevertheless, it was both fascinating and instructive. The wines were noted in a beautifully bound tasting book which was illustrated with hand-painted portraits of the leading tasters. In an equally substantial, hand-tooled, cowhide slip case was a matching bound copy of the Christie edition of Ray's 'Lafite'. It was quite an evening.

What motivated the good doctor? Not self-aggrandisement, but a rather American determination – aided by a large dose of Texan hospitality – to do something spectacularly well, and to provide a marvellous opportunity for his guests, selected for their tasting abilities and seriousness, to share his enthusiasm and to assess legendary vintages.

The first notable 'horizontal' tasting (several different châteaux of one vintage) took place in a small country town in Holland in May 1978. Planned and executed by a local doctor, it was a horizontal of 19 top Bordeaux châteaux of the 1961 vintage. Dr John Taam's aim, quite simply, was to see whether the reputation of the vintage was justified and to decide which châteaux held the most promise. He had invited a dozen or so friends and one or two professionals such as myself to be judge and jury. The wines were tasted blind to avoid bias. It was a very pleasant and instructive day.

Soon other collectors followed suit. The nucleus of wines was generally from their own cellars, with guests chipping in to fill the gaps, delivering bottles well in advance of the scheduled tasting to give the wine time to settle. Typically, to celebrate and assess their 20th anniversary, the modest, unassuming and generous Dr Louis Skinner hosted a horizontal tasting of 1961 clarets in 1981. It was for this tasting that he and I devised the system of serving wines in 'flights' at precise and quite speedy intervals, with review breaks in between. To avoid fatigue the tasting was in three sessions: Saturday morning, Saturday afternoon and Sunday morning. A similar programme was emulated by Robert Paul, Dr Skinner's neighbour in Coral Gables, Florida, at more recent tastings. First he held a horizontal of 1978 red Bordeaux and, the following year, an equally instructive horizontal of 96 châteaux from St-Emilion and Pomerol, all of the 1982 vintage. At the Skinner and Paul tastings, by serving two bottles of each wine and pouring alternately, bottle variation – which is encountered not infrequently, even with comparatively young vintages – can be more easily detected. Another recent and welcome development has been the presence of châteaux proprietors, for whom these tastings are a revelation as they have no parallel in France.

There are also semi-commercial tastings, the sort organized by Bipin Desai, a physicist, in Los Angeles. Desai purchases the wines over a long period and invites paying guests. I tend to sing for my supper at these events, acting as co-ordinator and commentator, and find them invaluable. Perhaps the most notable have been the verticals of Châteaux Margaux and La Mission-Haut-Brion, both attended by their respective proprietors, who found comparison of a large number of vintages most instructive.

Over the past few years German collectors have entered the field, and in their company I have encountered some of the very finest wines. Happily, as I speak no German, I can concentrate on tasting without distraction. Undoubtedly, 'the host with the most' is Hardy Rodenstock. I forget the date of the first of his annual tastings I attended, though everything else I remember all too well. It took place in a German country inn and guests assembled, in black ties, at 11.30 am for a welcoming glass (or two) of champagne. We sat down at 12 noon and, 72 wines and a six-course meal later, with only a short mid-afternoon break, arose at 12 midnight. I had a splitting headache and was very ill that night. The misery was not improved by having to get up at six am the following morning to catch an early flight from Dusseldorf to London to conduct a wine auction held "at 11 am precisely". The following year I took my own spittoon and, between wines, avoiding the rich food, consumed mainly bread and water!

Rodenstock's next spectacular was an all-day affair held at Château d'Yquem. The guests included the proprietor, Comte Alexandre de Lur Saluces, and several other French notables, and my customary solitary English representation was augmented by Jancis Robinson. Then came two weekend spectaculars, both held at a luxurious ski-resort hotel near the top of a pass in Austria. The entire hotel had been commandeered, and Rodenstock's guests were overwhelmed with a vast array of rare, often magnificent, and it must be admitted, one or two disappointing, aged wines. Each event, which takes nearly a year to organize, is a treasured experience.

My preference is for instructive verticals and I shall try to describe two. The first, a spectacular 116 vintages of Château Lafite from 1985 back to 1784, plus 11 old vintages of Carruades, was held in New Orleans in October 1988. This monumental tasting was given by Lloyd Flatt who, incidentally, was one of the guests at Dr Overton's original Lafite tasting. Lloyd's method is original and sensible. To avoid fatigue, his tastings are held in five sessions over three days. Each session consists of a 'flight' or group averaging six vintages, and, more significantly, these flights are arranged in related vintages and in such an order as to ensure that the greatest wines are served at a stage when our senses are most alert and palates least fatigued. For example, on the first morning, to get ourselves attuned, flight one consisted of the 1954, 1953, 1952, 1951 and 1950 vintages, 1953 naturally being the touchstone. Next was a leap into the past with a group of vintages rarely seen and therefore particularly interesting: 1902, 1903, 1904, 1905, 1906, 1907 and 1908, including the Carruades of Château Lafite 1902. There were some surprises here, particularly the 1905 and 1906, though the (single) bottles of 1903 and 1908 were sadly oxidized. For flight three, Flatt served the first group of the great pre-phylloxeras: 1868, 1869, 1870 and 1872. The rarely-seen 1868 was rich but dry; the 1869, a reliably big vintage, still magnificent; and the legendary 1870 as perfect, rich, and beautifully balanced as its reputation.

Even if I had the space, it would be tedious to describe all the flights. Suffice to say that during the course of this marathon event we tasted every vintage between 1864 and 1985, with the exception of 1866 and 1867, 1884 and 1885, 1901, 1909, 1915, 1930, 1932, 1935 and 1936. For good measure, we also tasted the 1844, 1846 and 1848, a marvellous trio; then the 1832 and 1806, both bought at Christie's and, happily, in superb condition, the latter light, elegant and delicious, the 1832 magnificent, and sound as a bell. Alas, the *pièce de résistance*, the 1787, recumbent in a Lear jet between Malibu and New Orleans, had half its contents syphoned out. All that remained was a most beautifully perfumed, intense, rich vinegar. A great pity, because the Mouton 1787 from the same cellar, opened a year or so previously at the château, had been incredibly good.

Château d'Yquem has been the subject of quite a few remarkable tastings, the most memorable that I have been connected with taking place in Chicago the day before a big Christie's wine auction. Just over 50 vintages were assembled by a private collector, Bud Moon. Between us we combined the two methods of tasting. There were eight flights, the first four in the afternoon, each of six vintages from 1983 back to 1956. The evening session opened with a flight of relatively poor vintages (1946, 1940, 1931, 1919, 1913 and 1912) followed by one of the very best (1949, 1947, 1945, 1937, 1929 and 1921) – each with its own character and all absolutely magnificent. The penultimate flight was of 19th-century vintages: 1892 oxidized, 1875 acetic, 1871 remarkably good. But the 1825 was the surprise of the day: a rich amber-tawny colour with a pronounced green rim, incredible fragrance, like ambrosial fruit salad; still sweet, concentrated and fig-like, with marvellous acidity and fabulous after-taste. The 1900 was good but overshadowed; the 1847, alas, a poor bottle. At a previous Rodenstock weekend I had rated the Yquem 1847 the most marvellous wine I had *ever* tasted. But that's the challenge of old wine. Some you win, some you lose.

Do tasters ever drink? Yes, of course, but it is foolish to drink through a long tasting – though I notice that the Germans never spit out. I make copious notes. As soon as the wine is put before me, I give it a twirl to coat the whole of the inside surface. Next, noting the precise time, assess the initial impact of the bouquet. Then back to the appearance, observing its colour, depth, and the gradation revealing the signs of maturity at the rim. I nose it again, and taste. After I have tasted and noted the entire flight, I look at the development of the bouquet in the glass through to its eventual fading. Why? Because for me the hallmark of a fine – a great – wine, is the way the bouquet evolves, blossoms and is retained over a period of time, and how its concentration, finesse and length develop on the palate. But I never lose sight of the principal purpose of the tasting, which is to assess the quality and stage of development of a wine of a particular vintage, making due allowance for bottle variation and the fallibility of corks.

For me, every tasting is a voyage of discovery.

Harrods Book of Fine Wine (1990)

I and sister are just returned from Paris! We have eaten frogs. It has been such a treat! You know our monotonous tenor. Frogs are the nicest little delicate things – rabbity-flavoured. Imagine a Lilliputian rabbit! They fricassé them; but in my mind, dressed seethed, plain, with parsley and butter, would have been the decision of Apicius.

CHARLES LAMB: *Letters*

"Did you know," the Savoy Hotel group writes to me "that Guy Burgess had his last lunch in England at Simpsons-in-the-Strand with his fellow conspirator Maclean before defecting to Russia?"

I didn't. Yet it was an interesting choice of restaurant on Burgess's part for he was something of a gourmet in his own way. In his flat in Bond Street, his friend Goronwy Rees noted, Burgess relied on "a very large, very heavy iron saucepan filled to the brim with a kind of thick grey gruel, compounded of porridge, kippers, bacon, garlic, onion and everything else that may have been lying about in his kitchen. This unappetising mess he had cooked for himself the previous day, and on it he proposed to subsist until Monday morning."

Kenneth Rose's 'Albany' column, *The Sunday Telegraph*, 14 May 1991

TALES OF EXCESS

"I THINK HE WAS KILLED . . ."

LAGER-LOUTERY DE LUXE

December 8, 1924: I am at the moment just recovering from a heavy bout of drinking. I had a good drinking evening with Alec, Terence, and Richard Greene. Exactly a week later I suddenly went to Oxford by the most impossible train which stopped at every station. I arrived at 10.30 and drove to 31 St Aldate's where I found an enormous orgy in progress. Billy and I unearthed a strap and whipped Tony. Everyone was hideously drunk except strangely enough myself.

Next day I moved to 40 Beaumont Street and began a vastly expensive career of alcohol. I had a dinner party. I arrived quite blind after a great number of cocktails at the George with Claud. Eventually the dinner broke up and Claud, Roger Hollis and I went off for a pub-crawl which after sundry indecorous adventures ended up at the Hypocrites where another blind was going on. Poor Mr Macgregor turned up after having lain with a woman but almost immediately fell backwards downstairs. I think he was killed.

Next day I drank all the morning from pub to pub. I ate no lunch but drank solidly. I then drank double brandies until I could not walk . . . I fell out of a window and then relapsed into unconsciousness punctuated with severe but well-directed vomitings. I dined four times at various places and went to a drunk party at Worcester in someone's rooms I did not know. On Wednesday I was sober.

Next day I lunched with Hugh [Lygon] and drank with him all afternoon and sallied out with him fighting drunk at tea-time when we drank at the New Reform until dinner.

Extract from *The Diaries of Evelyn Waugh, 1903–66* (1976)

MY LIFE AS A DRUNK

PETER LANGAN

It is said that the English disease is buggery, the German flagellation and the Irish drink. The Irish one probably protected me from the other two deviations due either to a lack of inclination or a horizontally inebriate condition.

Levity aside, never become an alcoholic like me. The pleasure wanes over the years and suffers a sea change into something weird and strange. The pleasure becomes a plague. If you like a drink, you cannot afford to become an alky. You either have to give it up or take a one-way ticket to your local cremmy.

Myself, I try to stop all the time but I often fall by the grapeside. The other morning in that limbo world between deep sleep and wide awake I heard a voice.

"Hey Langan! Can you hear me?"

"What? Yes. Yes, what is it? Who's there anyway?"

"It's me. I'm your liver."

"So what?"

"I'm going on strike. That's so what."

"Bugger off! I've got a hangover."

"Listen, Mr Langan. I'm no Arthur Scargill. If I go on strike, you go to the charcoal grill at Golders Green."

"What do you want?"

"Good living conditions and a year's sabbatical. Otherwise the lads – your balls, kidneys, heart and what's left of your brain – will pack in work and be gone. You're buggered old son!"

"OK. OK. When do I have to start?"

"Right now. Understood?"

I awake to the grim reality of alcoholic poisoning and three days of pain. There is no cure for alcoholic poisoning but there is a Langan Elixir which fixes any hangover. Forget those pseudo-cures you see hanging on straps in pubs. This is the definitive cure.

Directions: place dried apricots in a jam jar (or any other jar) until it is about a quarter full. Fill the jar with an amontillado-style medium sherry. Leave for a week. It is advisable to turn the jar upside down occasionally. This way each apricot gets to full bloom. The apricots will swell into round rich sodden beauties. The sherry takes the flavour of the fruit. In a week the nectar is ready. Make as much as you like. The alcohol means that it does not need to be re-frigerated but I prefer it that way. The morning after, a small glass of the nectar with no more than two of the apricots makes for a mix-ture which sets you up for the day. It is addictive and as the notice says on a cigarette pack – it can be dangerous to your health.

The apricots with a little of the nectar and some vanilla ice cream with slivers of toasted almonds make a superb instant dessert.

May 1991

VICTORIANA

LINES
WRITTEN FOR A FRIEND ON THE DEATH
OF HIS BROTHER, CAUSED BY A RAILWAY
TRAIN RUNNING OVER HIM WHILST HE
WAS IN A STATE OF INEBRIATION

How oft alas my brother have I warned thee to
    beware
The horrid spells of guilt which led the drunkard's
    life to *care*;
But no! you heeded not the warning words I spoke
    with pain,
Your wretched soul that once was pure was bound
    as in a chain;
At length, one cold October, when the night was
    late and dark,
The awful doom came on which sank thy life's
    unsteady barque;
Thy mangled corpse upon the rails in frightful shape
    was found,
The ponderous train had killed thee as its heavy wheel
    went round;
And thus in dreadful form thou met'st a drunkard's
    awful death,
And I, thy brother, mourn thy fate, and breathe a
    purer breath.

JAMES HENRY POWELL, *Phases of Thought and Feeling* (1857)

THE SPIRIT OF THE WINE

It got into the old man's mouth,
   It crept into his head;
It pinched his cheeks, it pinched his eyes,
   He felt them growing red:
It sat upon the old man's nose,
   It peeped out from his eyes,
Until he knew not this from that,
   The fish-pond from the skies.
Oh, a cunning little fellow is the Spirit of the Wine.

He trembles when he lies awake
   At night upon his bed:
It is the Spirit makes him ill,
   And soon he will be dead.
Oh, bid him put the wine away,
   And pray to be forgiven,
Or he will go from bad to worse,
   And never get to heaven:
And all because the old man loved the Spirit of the Wine.

'AUNT EFFIE'

Can you listen a heart-thrilling story
   Of pathos, and passion, and sin –
A Tale of the tragical sorrow
   That comes of the liking for gin?

ALEXANDER G. MURDOCH

Extracts from *The Book of Temperance Readings and Recitations*. Selected and arranged by the Rev. J. A. Jennings, M.A. Dublin (1886).

A TALE OF WOE

... who so happy as we,
As we'd sit of an eve, 'neath the old poplar tree,
And paint fairy pictures, of years yet in store,
And a future of bliss, how we'd vainly explore.

Ah! vainly indeed, for sad to relate,
My John's home returnings began to grow late,
And I learnt, as from business, he wended his way,
He was oft at the alehouse persuaded to stay.
This was not the worst, for I found by his pay
That he ofttimes would spend at the inn a whole day;
Thus his wages grew less, tho' his work it was good,
And 'twas rare that he brought me sufficient for food.
And thus things went on, nay, got steadily worse,
For poor John soon got fully enslaved to the curse.
He lost his employ, and, oh the disgrace!
My husband was now the whole talk of the place.
Our sweet little Nellie, who lies yonder there,
Had ev'n her sad part of this burden to share:
For her garments were thin, and her food it was scant,
In fact the dear baby was pining with want,
We got into debt, our home soon was sold,
Alas! all our misery could never be told,
Poor John, he fell ill; how I grieved for the man!
His form thin and wasted, his features how wan!
He died, but how sudden! we awoke in the morn,
My Nellie an orphan, I a widow forlorn;
No farewell he bade us, ere his spirit took flight;
The verdict, he died thro' strong drink in the night.

JAMES WARD, *Poems and Elegies* (1883)

FONDLY REMEMBERED

ROBERT BARNARD

"Would you like another cheese and onion twisty?" asked Annie Monkton from the passenger seat, pushing the bag in the direction of the steering-wheel.

"No, thanks, Ma, I'm happy with the prawn cocktail crisps," said her son Herbie, speeding up the M1, but brandishing the bag with his free hand.

"You like those, don't you? I like them now and *again* . . . "

"Have one, Ma."

"Ta, I don't mind if I do."

Her arm wobbled over towards the bag, and her elbow pushed itself companionably into her son's comfortable belly. Herbie was six foot three and seventeen stone, and Annie was five foot six and thirteen stone, so their bodies in the little Fiat were touching constantly. But they'd had many trips over the years in the small car, and had learnt to cope without friction.

"That was nice, for a change," said Annie, munching. "Tasty. Do you remember that seafood cocktail we had at the Monk's Head in Kendal that year?"

"How could I forget it?" said Herbie enthusiastically. "It was brilliant! It had everything: prawn, crab, cod, smoked haddock. It was Dad recommended that hotel."

"He was good on hotels, was your dad. He could be a miserable bugger, as you well know, but he knew his hotels. It was him having been a traveller, I suppose."

"Yes, you'd remember, wouldn't you, where you'd had a really good nosh-up, and where it hadn't come up to standard."

They sped through the county of Nottinghamshire, their eyes on the highway, except when they dropped to the bags in their hands.

"I've got some coconut ice in my handbag," said Annie. "Fancy a bit, son?"

"No, I think I'll stick with the smoked almonds."

They munched contentedly. Herbie was thinking.

"Do you remember that coconut ice we got in the market in Leeds last year – with all the glacé bits in, and the peel?"

"I do. It was scrumptious. I've often thought about that coconut ice."

"Now," said Herbie, when he had got his thoughts in order, "what I'm wondering is, are we going to stop for lunch at the White Hart in Hunstable, or at the Fox and Newt in Carditch? Or we could even try the Mayflower at Kirkby again."

"Is that the pub your father took us to? Said he'd had a marvellous rump steak there that nearly filled the plate? Then when he took us it was very disappointing. Mingy little portions, and tough at that, and hardly enough chips to feed a baby."

"It'd changed management."

"It had. They ought to warn people. I remember your dad after that meal. Hardly said a word all afternoon. No, thank you, we won't try there again. I won't be done twice over. Let's see, the White Hart's where they do that lovely steak and mushroom pie, isn't it?"

"That's right. Massive portions. With jacket potatoes with grated cheese on."

"Oh yes. I remember that. Melted in the mouth. And the Fox and Newt's where we had that lovely plaice and chips, where the chips were practically unlimited."

"That's right. I don't know when I've had better plaice and chips."

"Still, I fancy the steak and mushroom today. We'll have time to digest it before we have our dinner."

So they stopped at the White Hart, and it hadn't changed hands, and they had the steak and mushroom, and the potatoes with the melted cheese, and a very generous helping of boiled carrots, and Annie washed hers down with a gin and tonic, and Herbie washed his down with a pint of bitter. And just when they thought they'd finished, Herbie wondered whether he couldn't manage a piece of that Black Forest gâteau he'd seen at the food bar, and Annie wondered whether she couldn't too, and she said she'd buy another round of drinks to go with it, if Herbie would fetch them from the bar. So they had the gâteau too, and another round of drinks, and they were very pleased they did.

"That was lovely," Annie said. "That was almost as good as the Black Forest gâteau they serve at the King's Head in Shoreditch. You know, the one your dad always swore by."

"That's right. He loved his Black Forest gâteau, didn't he? We must go out to the King's Head again some time. We haven't been there since he died."

"Not since he had his Attack, in actual fact . . . I didn't like it after your dad had his Attack. I mean, we couldn't get around like we'd been used to, could we? . . . Still I must say that gâteau we've just had was almost as good, and a very nice-sized portion too. That should keep us going until dinner."

As they went towards the car, Annie said:

"Even your dad would have been satisfied with that meal. Walter was always less snappy when he'd really got his money's worth, wasn't he?"

They opened the boot, and Annie got out her large holdall and took from it a supersize bar of fruit and nut, some liquorice comfits, and a bag of bacon munchies. Herbert took a packet of potato sticks and a tin of cashews, because, as he said, he'd had enough sweet things for the moment. They drove on, out of Nottinghamshire and into Yorkshire, perfectly happy.

"I like Yorkshire," said Annie. "They always do you proud in Yorkshire."

"They know how to appreciate food in the North," said Herbie.

"They do. You can see it in the people."

"The question is," said Herbie, lighting up a cigarette between the potato sticks and the cashews, "are we going to drive on up to the Lake District tonight, or are we going to stop off in Yorkshire somewhere?"

"Oh, I thought we'd agreed. Stop off. No point in overdoing it. We're not in a race. We've got the whole weekend, and we don't have to be home till Monday night. There's lots of lovely hotels in Yorkshire where they always make you ever so welcome. There's Manor Court, just outside Ilkley, where they do that marvellous table d'hôte for six pounds fifty a head . . ."

They talked over the various alternatives, and finally decided to save Manor Court for the Sunday on the way back, and to spend the night at the Devonshire Arms in Spenlow. They enjoyed a pre-dinner lager and lime in the bar while they went through the menu. Finally Herbie ordered the smoked salmon, followed by sirloin steak with French fries, while Annie ordered the seafood platter, followed by fillet of pork Wellington. Herbie had a pint of bitter at table, and Annie a snowball, and they were as near as possible in a state of perfect bliss until Annie, over the pork Wellington, which as she happily observed nearly covered the plate, suddenly remembered something.

"Here," she said, "it's just come to me. The Devonshire Arms was the last place we ever stayed at with your dad. Last trip we ever had. We stayed here at the Devonshire Arms on the way down from Skye and the Western Isles."

"Did we, Ma? I'd never have remembered that."

"Well, you should. Three days later he had his first Attack."

"I remember it was soon after we'd got back from somewhere."

"And do you know what he had for his dinner that night? Fillet of pork Wellington!"

For a moment the remembrance of things past seemed to cast a shadow over the meal. Annie looked at the great expanse of pork that had been set before her, and she gave the dead Walter the tribute of a passing sigh. Then she took a sip of her snowball, smiled at her son, and set to with a will again.

"Doesn't do to take things like that, does it?" she said.

"Thinking won't bring him back," said Herbie.

So they didn't think about him.

Next morning they had an English breakfast of egg, bacon, sausage, tomatoes, mushrooms and fried potatoes, with the Yorkshire addition of black pudding, which Herbie pronounced "not bad, but I don't think I'd want it as a regular thing". He considered the porridge excellent, though, especially with the golden syrup over, and Annie gave her blessing to the marmalade.

"It's my big criteria," she said, "to tell a good hotel from a second-rater. That's none of your cheap stuff —" and she waved her pudgy hand at the pot – "because there's no question of skimping here."

When they'd paid their bill, Herbie humped their luggage to the car – just the one small case, because Herbie hated lugging heavy cases, and considered it shortened your life span – and they set off again.

"People are silly, giving up good English breakfasts," said Annie as they drove out of the hotel drive. "They set you up for the day."

She slipped into her mouth a piece of chocolate nougat and chewed contentedly.

"That meal last night," she said, "the pork Wellington, would have been one of the last good meals your dad ever ate. Apart from the ones I cooked him, of course. The *very* last meal he ate out. He liked eating out, your dad. I never knew a better judge of whether he'd had value for money."

"Wasn't any point in him eating out, not after his Attack," said Herbie. "Not with the sort of stuff he was allowed to eat."

"No. Imagine going into an Italian restaurant and saying 'I want a nice piece of boiled fish, and some boiled potatoes to go with it.' They'd have split their sides laughing."

"I don't think Dad had the *heart* to eat out again," said Herbie.

"That's it. It was funny, really. Do you remember that mini-cruise we took to Norway – ooh, back in '70 or '71 it must have been – and how Dad hated all that boiled fish and boiled potatoes we had? It was boiled potatoes with every meal, wasn't it? Just the most uninteresting way of having potatoes, *I* always say. Your dad was really disgusted, considering the price we'd paid. And then when he comes out of hospital, to have to have boiled fish and boiled potatoes and all that horrible invalid food. It was almost as if the doctor who drew up the diet sheet knew about Dad's likes and dislikes, and was trying to get his own back . . . Because your dad was not an easy patient . . . Short-tempered . . ."

"Well, you was very good to him, Ma. You cooked it all for him, didn't you?"

"I did, though it turned my stomach sometimes, quite apart from the extra work. I mean, the only thing we could've eaten that was on his diet was the shepherd's pie, and he wasn't to have that more than once a week. So there was his little messes to do, on top of the things for ourselves . . . It was pitiful watching him eating it . . ."

"And watching *him* watching *us*, eh, Ma?"

Annie Monkton gurgled a little laugh.

"Well, he *was* a picture, I'll give you that. But I still think it was diabolical, that diet sheet. It can't have been necessary. I'm no doctor, but I do know a grown man's got to eat enough to keep body and soul together. To see him sitting there with his pea soup, and the rusk he was suppose to have with it, while we were tucking in to the steak pizzaiola with the sauté potatoes and the baked aubergines – well, I said at the time it wasn't right."

"I think it was the sweets that got him most, Ma. That Peach Melba you used to make, with the thick whipped cream and the black cherry jam on top. He used to look at that, gaze you might say, like he was transfixed, like he begrudged us every mouthful . . . We haven't had your Peach Melba lately, have we, Ma?"

"Here, don't go so fast," said Annie, as they sped along the shores of Lake Windermere. "We don't want to get to Keswick too early for lunch."

They both had fresh salmon for lunch, with French fries, peas and beans. "You pay for Scottish salmon," said Herbie, "but it does have that touch of class." The thought of how much they'd paid for the salmon made them shake their heads reluctantly over the cheese and walnut gâteau. Afterwards they both had a little nap in the car park of the Keswick hotel where they'd eaten, and then Herbie got out his map and they decided where to stay for the night, nibbling at a little bag of savoury sticks. It was a question of whether to go over to Buttermere and then on to the coast and stay at Whitehaven, or whether to take a leisurely trip around Ullswater and overnight at Penrith.

"I'd go for Penrith," said Annie. "The Borderer at Penrith. I've got a fancy to try their venison again. I know it's extravagant, but we *are* on holiday."

Annie had woken from her nap with her mind greatly refreshed.

"Do you know," she said as they started, "I don't think they put as much fruit in fruit and nut chocolate as they used to. Or as much nut, come to that."

"That's the way the cookie crumbles," said Herbie, not altogether appositely.

They drove along the north shores of Ullswater, passing as they did so, though without seeing them, several hosts of golden daffodils.

"This is a good road now," said Herbie, increasing the speed. "A sight better than when we first came up, eh, Ma? Then you really had to dawdle round, because of the potholes."

But his mother's mind was on other things.

"I didn't *really* enjoy your father's gazing at us eating, like he used to after his Attack," she said, switching from the fruit and nut to the peppermint fondant. "I'm not cruel, you know that, Herbie. In fact, though it was a bit of a laugh at first, after a time I found it really put me off my food. Being watched like that. I just wasn't enjoying it any more. I remember sitting there eating a slice of one of my homemade pork pies – with all that lovely jelly, just as I like it – and your dad was toying with his omelette and looking at my plate greedily (because, not to speak ill of the dead, he could be greedy, your dad), and I thought: I can't enjoy this like I should be doing, not with him looking on like he wanted to grab every forkful from me. It was as much as I could do to finish it."

"Perhaps he should have ate separately, Ma."

"That would have been like putting him into an insulation ward. No, no, we was a family, and we ate as a family . . . I must say I was glad when they said he could start relaxing the diet."

Herbie shifted into lower gear up a hill, and dipped into his bag of salt and vinegar flavoured crisps.

"I think they meant gradually, Ma."

"Well, of course! That was how we went, wasn't it? The whole of the first week we hardly changed his old diet at all. I just gave him a bit of stewed apple or a tiny bit of jam roly-poly for afters. I said to him, I said: 'Keep well *under* for the first few days, then you can go *over* on Sunday, have a bit of a blow-out.'"

Herbie was quiet for a bit, then he said:

"Well, he enjoyed it, I will say that."

"Oh, he did. He'd been looking forward to it all week. You could feel the juices running. We talked it all over, you know. There was the lobster pâté, which was his favourite as starters, with the little fingers of buttered toast. Then there was the pork steaks with the mushroom cream sauce that he loved, and the scalloped potatoes and the glazed carrots and the cauliflower in cheese sauce. Then there was the Madeira chocolate cake with the sherry cream topping – the one I got the recipe for out of *Woman's Own*. We'd planned it all. It was a lovely meal."

"A meal fit for a king," admitted Herbie.

"And I didn't make any trouble over cooking it, though none of it was convenience foods. I had to do it all with my own hands, but it was a pleasure to me to do it. I loved cooking it for him."

"And he loved eating it," said Herbie. "Even the chocolate cake."

"Well, it was the best I'd ever made. I thought so myself when I ate up the rest the next day. It was perfection. Maybe it was *so* good that in a way he . . . couldn't stand it."

"It wasn't a bad way to go," said Herbie.

"It was a very *good* way to go. I hope I go like that when my time comes. And it was quick too. We'd hardly got him upstairs into the bed before he was gone. A darned sight better than lingering, that's what *I* say."

"It's what I'd call a good death."

"So would I. And I'd have been almost happy about it, if it hadn't been for that bleeding doctor," said Annie, getting almost agitated, and taking out of her handbag a tiny handkerchief, which she dabbed at her eyes.

"Dr Causeley?" said Herbert, surprised. "He never said anything out of turn in the bedroom."

"No. It was when he came downstairs. I never told you this, son, because I thought it would make you wild. I'd gone downstairs, being upset, to have a bit of a weep by the fire in the dining-room. And he came downstairs and he came in, and he was just starting to say something when – well, you see, the plates with the sweets was still on the table, with his bit of chocolate cake still unfinished, which had gone to my heart when I came in, and he saw that, and he saw the other plates which was piled on the sideboard, and he looked at them – *inspected* I'd call it, in a thoroughly nasty way that he'd no call to adopt – and he said had he been eating this? and I said yes, and explained we'd been sort of saving up on the calories, so he could have one good blow-out. And he said, 'What exactly did he have?' and so I told him. And do you know what he said?"

"No, Ma. What did he say?"

"He said: 'That meal killed him as surely as if you'd laced it with strychnine.'"

Herbie didn't go wild, but he thought for a bit.

"That wasn't very nice of him."

"It was diabolical. You could have knocked me down with a feather! Me just widowed not five minutes since."

"It was a liberty. These professional people take too much on themselves."

"They do. Your dad always said that. It was a wicked, cruel thing to say. And you notice he never had any doubt about signing the death certificate ... That's why I changed my doctor ... I never could fancy going back to Dr Causeley after that ... I know I haven't got anything to reproach myself with ..."

They went quiet for a bit, and Annie Monkton found a sucky sweet in her bag and comforted herself with that. Quite soon they were drawing up in the courtyard of the Borderer. Herbie got out, and made sure they'd got rooms. Luckily the tourist season was only just beginning. He came back smiling.

"Couldn't be better. Two nice singles. I took a peek at the dinner menu, Ma. You'll be able to have the venison. I've worked up an appetite, so I think I'm going to fancy the mixed grill."

As he took the case from the boot and they started towards the main door, Annie's good humour returned. She nudged Herbie with her fat arm.

"It's nice being on our own, though, isn't it, son?"

First published as 'Blown Up' in *Death of a Salesperson* (1989)

"I said to Lord Melbourne that I could not bear to hear that he thought so much of eating and drinking – it is *low* to think of such things."

QUEEN VICTORIA

Pork made him ill, he once informed the queen, after a night of indigestion, but he never liked to own it. "What makes you own it now?" asked she. "A fit of conscience," sighed Lord Melbourne.

DAVID CECIL: *Lord Melbourne*

THREE MEN IN A CLUB

ELIZABETH RAY

Do gambling and gastronomy always go together? Certainly during the short life (1828–44) of Crockford's Club, haunt of Regency Bucks, peers, sportsmen and men-about-town, the two seemed to go hand in hand; and three characters, all connected in one way or another, stand out for their appreciation of good living, and for the way money passed through their hands.

Throughout the 19th century clubs were very prominent in the life of London's West End, their chefs almost as well-known as their members. The most renowned of all was Alexis Soyer, chef of the Reform, but a few years earlier his older friend and compatriot, Louis Eustache Ude, was the darling of clubland when he was chef to Crockford's. He was succeeded, in turn, by Francatelli, one-time chef to Queen Victoria.

Two of the habitués of Crockford's during Ude's reign were the Second Earl of Sefton, described by a contemporary as "a gigantic hunchback" and nicknamed 'The Pet', who had employed Ude as his own chef, given him a pension of £300 a year, and continued to enjoy his cooking at Crockford's; and the Second Baron Alvanley, a few years younger, unkindly referred to as "a bloated buffoon" – a slur over which he fought a duel – but said to be the wittiest man of his time. Alvanley lodged at Ude's house, not far from the club, and although Ude was noisy and constantly quarrelling with his wife, Alvanley the gourmet considered the advantages of living under the same roof as the chef too great to miss.

Not a great deal is known about the early life of Ude, except that, as he writes in the preface to his book *The French Cook*, "through the unsettled temper" of his father he was apprenticed to a number of trades: printer, ladies' hairdresser, jeweller, engraver, until he had to learn "in a hurry" the art of cookery, in order to keep the family. He succeeded his father in a position at Court, which suggests that he too was a chef. Perhaps a gambler, as well, for the family seemed always to be in difficulties.

Ude united his gastronomy with gambling early on. After the French Revolution had destroyed his calling as a chef – all the aristocratic patrons who had survived had left Paris – he became the superintendent of a gambling house. After this he became a speculator – of limited success it appears – on the Bourse. None of his employments seemed to last very long, and he is always vague as to the reason ("circumstances forced me to leave . . . "), so perhaps the gambling had the upper hand. He became chef to Letitia Bonaparte, the mother of Napoleon, but he said that she was too parsimonious for him to continue long in her service.

However, the time Ude spent with Madame Bonaparte gave him "many opportunities of being acquainted with the secrets of the Cabinet", and he was able to dine "sometimes with dukes and princes, at others with *parvenus, filles entretenues*, actresses, gamblers, &c." But before he went to Crockford's he worked for Lord Sefton, creating many dishes that he named after his patron. These dishes, though very popular at the time, seem now to be completely forgotten. Who now makes Sefton Fancies, Veal Custard à la Sefton, Sefton puddings and, most popular of all, Sefton Patties, or *timballe de laitance de Maquereau à la Sefton* (mackerel roes in a pastry case), a dish Lord Sefton claimed to have devised himself?

Sefton was much liked, a friend of the Prince Regent (though there was later a falling-out), an active Whig politician, a noted epicure and a dedicated gambler both at cards and on horses. He broke the bank at Crockford's two nights running, and on another occasion lost £10,000. He was a founder-member of the Four-in-Hand Club, which was devoted to driving beautiful horses, with gleaming harnesses and well-kept carriages. Though a very dashing institution – all its members were grand gentlemen or peers – it was, according to the reminiscences of Captain Gronow (nicknamed Nogrow owing to his lack of inches), a thoroughly well-conducted affair, one of the club rules being that "no coach should pass another, and the pace should never exceed a trot". Sefton always drove bay horses, and also designed a special carriage known as the Sefton landau, with curved sides instead of the usual straight.

He took his eating and drinking very seriously. According to Creevy, that mine of information on matters of the time (and thought to be Sefton's illegitimate half-brother), breakfast seemed to be of the first importance. There would be four silver covered dishes on the table, one containing kidneys, another mashed potatoes, a third three partridges and trimmings of bread sauce and "crums", and finally a dish of "patties" – probably the famous mackerel roes. Another day the dishes might contain mutton cutlets, mashed potatoes, an "omlet" and a pheasant. "Now r-a-ally," wrote Creevy, "I think that is *trop*, is it not?"

The food at Crockford's was renowned everywhere. Crockford himself (known as 'the fishmonger' because of his earlier calling) was to be seen "seated snug and sly" at his desk, ever watchful as to what went on, and giving credit only to those he approved. One of these was certainly Sefton; when he died, he was said to have owed 'the fishmonger' £40,000, a debt paid reluctantly by his heir. Members were charged a modest sum for their dinners, and nothing for their wines, which encouraged them to frequent the gaming rooms, out of which the club made its money. Ude played his part fully:

Oh! 'tis a dazzling sight to see
The spread of thy festivity!
Those *petits pâtés* made so natty
For which the heart beats *pit-a-patty*
Thine omelettes *aux confitures*
Which no one elsewhere can endure:
Thine *asperges*, too, *en petits pois*
Which UDE can only, *sur ma foi*,
Dress up in that delicious way
Which ever marks his *entremets*.

. . .

Scarcely could the gourmand wish,
Or imagine any dish,
But 'twas here, at the command
Of his eager eyes and hand.
While Champagne, in close array,
Pride of *Rheims* and *Epernay*,
Not in bottles, but in dozens,
(Think of *that*, ye country cousins!)

There is much more of this deathless poetry, but that will suffice to give a little of the flavour of Crockford's and its chef.

All was not sweetness and light for Ude, though. One official complaint to the Committee mentioned "an admixture of onion in the *soubise*", and another member refused to pay an extra sixpence for the special sauce that accompanied the red mullet. Such things sent Ude into a towering rage, and once, when giving a birthday dinner at home, he was beside himself with anger. On this occasion one of his guests stumbled over one of the many dogs of the household (there were a number of dogs, cats and parrots) and knocked over a plate and the wine cooler, while another guest trod on a dog's paw, causing a noisy commotion. Then the guest appointed to carve the meat managed to break seven precious plates by putting them on the spirit warmer, while another diner not partial to venison fed the dogs under the table, causing a particularly greedy dog to choke to death, after which "the harmony of the evening was thus much disturbed." The final disaster was discovered later when the male guests rose to leave, only to discover that the dogs had licked all the polish from their boots.

History does not record whether Lord Alvanley was at home in his lodgings above the Ude household that night, or perhaps he was one of those invited. He was possibly hiding away from his creditors, of which there were so many that he had his door-knocker removed. He could never understand why the duns kept bothering him when they knew he had no money and only lived on credit.

Alvanley was highly intelligent, and had a reputation for great kindness and charm as well as for his wit. However, after a brief career in the Coldstream Guards, he did nothing with his life except spend money in a most profligate way, and enjoy the pleasures of both the gaming and the dining table. He frequently visited Brighton, and on one occasion, when asked how long he intended to stay, replied "Five and thirty pounds"; he thus reckoned on £10 for posting to and from London, leaving him "a pony" to spend, and as long as this lasted he would stay – probably for two more dinners and breakfasts at the York Hotel.

One of his continuing extravagances was to insist on having a fresh apricot tart on his sideboard every day of the year, and he recorded with pleasure a dinner he had of "Lambs' tails as big as muffins and head as small as French rolls, boiled with Egyptian onions and agro-dolce sauce of lemons and fresh sugar-cane".

Always given to the extravagant, he organised a dinner at which each guest was to provide the most expensive dish he could conceive, the winner to dine free. Alvanley's own contribution was a fricassee made only of the *noix* – the small bits from the back of a bird – for which about three hundred snipe, woodcock, pheasant and other tasty birds were used, the dish costing over £100. Another time he ordered an omelette made from peacock sausages and the eggs of the golden pheasant. He was also forgetful enough to order a £200 picnic hamper from Gunters for a river outing – and leave it behind.

Popular as he was, he must have been a worrying house-guest. His usual way of extinguishing his bedside candle was to fling it into the middle of the room throwing a pillow after it if it remained still alight, or simply putting the lighted candle straight under his pillow while lying in bed.

Both Sefton and Alvanley were members of Brooks's and White's as well as Crockford's, and, living nearby, their lives must have centred on St James's and its clubs. Alvanley was one of the famous and elite Bow-window Set at White's, the best-known being Brummell. They were called such after the window overlooking St James's Street, where they would sit "watching", as one put it, "the damn people get wet".

It may have been the shape of the window that gave them their name, but, considering the amount of food they put away, it might well have referred to their own outlines.

AN AWFUL WARNING

My soul is dark with stormy riot
Directly traceable to diet . . .

ANON

ENVOI

(Being monitory lines delivered to schoolboy son during his first Eton society dinner ...)

Let me tell you the think that I've thunk –
If you're drinking too much you'll be drunk:
So whilst you are drinking
Try not to get stinking,
For if stinking you'll stink like a skunk ...

And be warned by the wink that I've wunk –
No need to be meek as a monk,
But I trust you'll be able
To rise from the table
And find your way home to your bunk ...

For this is the fear that I funk –
That if in a stupor you're sunk
You'll be buzzed by the fuzz,
In a way the fuzz does,
And that then into clink you'll be clunk ...

CYRIL RAY

PITT AND PORT

Mr. Rogers has left these reminiscences of the statesman's port-drinking: "During his boyhood, Pitt was very weakly; and his physician, Addington (Lord Sidmouth's father), ordered him to take port wine in large quantities; the consequence was, that when he grew up he could not do without it. Lord Grenville has seen him swallow a bottle of port in tumblerfuls before going to the House. This, together with his habit of eating late suppers (indigestible cold veal pies, &c.), helped, undoubtedly, to shorten his life. Huskisson, speaking to me of Pitt, said that his hands shook so much that, when he helped himself to salt, he was obliged to support the right hand with the left. Stothard, the painter, happened to be one evening at an inn on the Kent Road, when Pitt and Dundas put up there on their way from Walmer. Next morning, as they were stepping into their carriage, the waiter said to Stothard, "Sir, do you observe these two gentlemen?" "Yes," he replied, "and I know them to be Mr. Pitt and Mr. Dundas." "Well, sir, how much wine do you suppose they drank last night?" Stothard could not guess. "Seven bottles, sir!"

ANON

TOMBSTONES

MALTA

Here lies John Tyrwitt
A learned divine
He died in a fit
Through drinking port wine

April 3rd 1828
Aged 39 years

KING'S STANLEY

'Twas as she tript from cask to cask
In at a bung-hole she quickly fell
Suffocation was her task
She had no time to say farewell

Ann Collins, died 11th September 1864
Aged 49

UN HOMME DE TABLE

JULIAN CRITCHLEY

Cyril Ray was more than a trencherman; he was *un homme de table*. I know there is a phrase in French *homme du monde*, and he was certainly that, too, but I should admit I am not sure of the provenance of *homme de table*. It could be that I have made it up. If so, then it would be as incomprehensible and ridiculous to the French as *cul de sac* ('a bag's arse') the description we use for what a French call *impasse*, a good example of Ministry of Transport's French. Never mind, the point about Cyril Ray was that he was a civilised man who used food and drink not simply to recruit himself, but to entertain. He would have been at his best in the Members' Dining Room of the House of Commons, breaking bread with his peers. Sadly, he was never elected.

Had he been an MP, and he certainly would not have been a Tory, Cyril would have adapted quickly to the two dicta of public life, which are, respectively, Powell's Law and Critchley's Law. Enoch Powell, who is a clever chap, although difficult at times, once said that humbug was the essential lubricant of public life. He was only partly right. My law says that gossip has an equally important part to play in politics, providing, as it does, the grease that facilitates conversation.

I hope that I am not about to betray any confidences or shock any readers, the more simple of whom might imagine that whenever two politicians, of whatever party, are gathered together, the subject of their conversation ranges from the Exchange Rate Mechanism to the Rate Support Grant and back. That will be the day. In fact, politicians rarely talk politics. Indeed, some of us go to the trouble of forming dining clubs such as the One Nation or the '92' to do precisely that.

There was a Victorian saw, repeated, I believe, in the earlier editions of Mrs Beeton, that 'gentlemen' spoke about ideas, and servants, people. If that is still true, then politicians are no gentlemen, not even members of the Labour Party. Put a plate, knife and fork, and, more particularly, a glass, before us, and we gossip like washerwomen. It is not so much who is sleeping with whom; despite the Ashdowns, Clintons, Stonehouses and Profumos, love is not what politicians do best. We are either too old, or too young, or, more likely, too busy. And we are too much in love with ourselves to waste time in dalliance. It is not love, but who is climbing the greasy poll, and more to the point, who is slipping down it, that interests us most.

Politics is the most competitive of all callings, even more so than the church. In no other trade is the rise and fall of its practitioners charted quite so publicly. Actors can rest, but we are simply defeated. Ministers of the Crown rise like comets only to vanish out of sight in a puff of smoke. What better pleasure is there for elderly backbenchers who have sat long and seen everything, to sit at lunch or dinner, shaking their grey heads over the misfortunes of their younger colleagues? We live on a diet of Sachertorte and *schadenfreude*, a mild pleasure at the news of the misfortunes of others, salting a diet which could best be described as 'filling'. What goes better with a dish of steak and kidney than the news of the fall from grace of some 'young meteor'?

We have been known to take a modest pleasure in the misfortunes of others, but in this we are probably no different from anybody else. Journalists rarely have a good word for other journalists, and with ample justification. But politicians are more charitable than parsons, less bitchy, perhaps, than lawyers. Let a Minister of the Crown go on late-night Irish television and sing, and we will say that we knew all along that he was tone deaf. Let a junior minister get pinched at a party conference for drink-driving, and we tell each other that "there but for the grace of God . . ." Let a politician's lawyers' safe be blown, and we determine never again to put pen to paper. Parliament is an arena where 650 schoolboys are encouraged to do their own thing, and to do it in full view of the nation. As with world championship ice-skating, the occasional pratfall is very welcome indeed.

Politicians are never at their best on their feet. Put a chair under them and they sparkle like a bottle of Jeffrey Archer's Krug. To get the full flavour of the Palace of Varieties you must lunch, take tea, or dine in the company of MPs. After Prime Minister's Questions on Tuesday and Thursday afternoons, the tea room fills rapidly with MPs eager to discuss the merits of his performance. Did Neil go on even longer than usual? Was John Major a paler shade of grey? When Mrs Thatcher was in trouble she would come into the tea room, flanked by bodyguards. The ambitious would sit to attention; the world weary, however, would make their excuses and leave. At lunch we wonder whatever happened to Edwina Currie, about whom tongues were once never still.

At dinner, the older hands will recall the details of the Cecil Parkinson affair when hell had no fury, and Mrs Thatcher kept a stiff upper lip. Still older hands will remember 'Jolly Jack' Profumo, whose poolside dalliance helped to bring down the Macmillan government. Those who were 'smart' enough to be in the know, blamed the then Chief Whip, Martin Redmayne, for allowing the wool to be pulled over his eyes. Things, we tell each other, are not what they used to be.

After the news of Paddy Ashdown's brief affair with his secretary broke weeks before the election, an elderly Knight of the Shires, who has since retired to his estates in the Midlands, suggested at dinner that all MPs' secretaries be vetted by a committee of 'senior Members' before being allowed to take up their employment. There were mutters of "hear, hear". He told us that at his public school, a lifetime or more ago, the housemaster made it his business to 'interview' all females who might have wished to seek employment as cook, maid or bottle-washer. He had two criteria for employment: age and an aggressive plainness. "He ran no risks, and nor should we" was Sir John's judgment. I am sorry to say that there is a tendency among the younger MPs to employ quite young women, who can be glimpsed every afternoon hanging on their employer's every word. My own secretary has her own bus pass, and was once employed by the Royal Borough of Kensington and Chelsea as a Traffic Warden.

Of course, if you believe that, you will believe anything. Gossip is not often inter-party, and Cyril, were he ever to have been elected, would have dined with members of his own party. In the Commons'

Dining Room we practise a curious culinary apartheid. We wash our own dirty linen. But were a Scottish Labour front bencher of immense rectitude to have been discovered dancing naked on a table during a Ladies' Night at the Caledonian Club, I cannot pretend that we Tories would permit the affair to go unremarked. We would simply buy a better bottle and say "I told you so". By the same token, Labour MPs would derive great pleasure from the revelation in the columns of the *Church Times* of a transvestite cabinet minister singing in a Hamburg night club. They would consider it further evidence of the Tory Party's fundamental unfitness to govern. Just imagine what a meal Gerald Kaufman would make of it. The point I am trying to make is that unless the 'scandal' is of considerable proportion, parliamentary gossip homes in on members of one's own political party. Tories gossip about Tories ("Heard what's happened to Harry? Never liked him"), Labour about Labour, and Liberals about everyone.

Much of the time we talk idly of our friends and passionately about our enemies, who are to be found in our own party. We complain of the tedium of long hours spent hanging around waiting for the liberating bell, and the rival merits of the 'cockup' and conspiracy theories one or the other of which underlie the frequent misfortunes of our colleagues. We are happy at Westminster. What is so dreadful about fighting elections is not only are we robbed of our creature comforts, but, marooned in our constituencies, we are cut off from the wider world. No longer are we the first to learn what it is than Ron Brown has got up to, or with what editor of a great family newspaper Pamella Bordes is passing the time of day. But a telephone call to our parliamentary secretary will keep us vividly in touch, for there are no secrets from her. We may look for the bodies, but it is the secretaries in the Commons who know where they are buried.

I have eaten lunch and dinner in the Commons for a quarter of a century. Robert Maxwell pinched our wine, and the food is just how mother made it, but we have had the advantage of being well-informed. I am sorry Cyril Ray never enjoyed a political career; we would have taken such pleasure in putting him in the picture. And he would have made a superb Chairman of the Commons' Catering Committee.

SPANISH
INTERLUDE

AN ANDALUSIAN TALE

LAURIE LEE

On our way back from Triana, up the street of the Catholic Kings, we looked for a tavern to rest ourselves, and found one called 'Pepito'. It was a lucky chance, for the proprietor was a prodigious epicure, loose-tongued and free-handed. His name was Antonio. He was a bald, youngish man, with a smooth face, shining eyes, stubby ring-covered fingers, and the greasy plumpness that comes from standing long hours behind a bar eating and drinking and waiting for customers. It was his own bar, and he was his own master, and the days were his own to make as pleasant as possible. Seldom, then, did he keep his ringed fingers from picking the food, his fat lips from tasting the many wines of the house. He was an enthusiast, an obsessive, and as soon as we arrived he began to offer us, without charge, glasses of wine from every barrel in the place.

"Approve this," he would say, banging a new one down on the counter and drawing off a little one for himself. Then, as one drank, he would step back a couple of paces, and stand, head on one side, like a painter observing his canvas. "You like it? Solera *buena*. You're right. It's no good. Approve this, then. Oloroso. Very rich. There you are." And bang came another glass, golden as honey, but set down with such force that half of it jumped out on to the floor.

So it went on. For two hours we approved. And for two hours he joined us, glass for glass, sipping holily, watching our eyes while we drank, and telling the history of the wine.

"This is a miracle. Approve the colour. With this you could suckle a baby. So kind it is. With this you could wash the dead and they'd resurrect themselves. Is stupendous, eh?"

And with every new glass Antonio would bawl to his wife, who was hidden behind a screen, and bid her fry some fresh tit-bit to eat with the wine. Great barrels were piled along the walls, chalked in red with their redolent names: Coñac, Manzanilla, Fino, Tinto, Amontillada, Blanca la Casa, Solera and Especial. We had a glass from each barrel, and from the best, several. If one was not emptied before the next was offered it was tossed airily into the street. And with every glass came some new delicious morsel, cooked by the invisible wife; fried fish, fried birds, kidneys, prawns, chopped pork, octopus, beans and sausage.

Antonio was the fat host of a golden age, persuasive, open-fisted, and delighted with our appetites. He cheated himself frivolously for the pleasure of seeing us drink. He talked all the time, and showed us photographs of himself going right back to his mother's breast. And from what we could see the years had hardly changed him at all.

Bewitched by this hospitality, we returned to Antonio another night. We had learned that it was his daughter's birthday, and we brought her cakes. When I placed the parcel on the counter he struck his head with his hand.

"I pollute the house!" he cried, rolling his eyes. "What sympathy. What grace." He bawled to his wife, who immediately began frying. Then he shouted upstairs to his daughter, María, to wash her face and put on fresh ribbons and come down and not dishonour him.

"I pollute the house," he cried again, looking at the cakes in amazement.

His daughter appeared, beautiful and dignified as an *infanta*, and shook our hands. It was her twelfth birthday. She talked to us solemnly about geography and arithmetic, while her father ripped out the corks of special bottles, prised open tins of ham and tunny fish, sent out for cigars, and spread the whole feast before us. And thus we gorged together till after midnight. Antonio was in a frenzy of pleasure, drunk with generosity, riotous and noisy as though at a wedding. María remained cool, courtly, soft spoken and rather prim. But the wife, endlessly frying behind the screen, never appeared at all.

Extract from *A Rose for Winter* (1955)

THE ROYAL RITZ

CHARLES HENNESSY

There used to be one in every great city. You used to arrive not in packaged groups but discreetly ushered by Mr Thos Cook, armed not with credit cards but with bankers' drafts, in sterling, which was as good as gold. You went by great transcontinental train, cosseted in Pullmans or wagons-lits, by ocean liner, or by Bentley, Delahaye or Hispano-Suiza, with miles of snooty bonnet and boxy boot. You were on the tail end, had you but known it, of the grand tour, and your destination, wherever you were headed, was a grand hotel.

Some of those great institutions, like Shepheard's in Cairo, are long gone. Some, like the St George in Beirut, have been compromised by events. Some, having lingered as shadows of their old selves, are to be born again: Raffles in Singapore, re-fitting for re-opening soon. But one, at least, seems to have been untouched by time and trouble, although it started with the undoubted advantage over its rivals of having been commanded by a king and created by the prince of hoteliers. It is the Ritz in Madrid and it stands, gleaming white in the Spanish sun, prow-like on its priceless corner site, fresh as it must have looked when Alfonso XIII opened it in 1910, a year when you knew everything would last forever.

The location is what impresses first. For any hotel, being next door to the Prado, arguably the world's greatest museum, would be enough. But the Ritz is jostled by the stock exchange and parliament too, not to mention the monumental central post office. If you feel hemmed in by such grandeur, the botanical gardens are nearby and, just up the street, is that most elegant of parks, the Retiro (retiring place). But hemmed in is the last thing you will feel in the Ritz, Madrid: what it has more of than perhaps any other grand hotel is space, an oasis at the smart hub of this great and busy city.

Alfonso (grandfather of the present king) was a much-travelled, cosmopolitan man, familiar with Edwardian London and most of the aristocratic watering-holes of Europe. But in 1906, when he got down to planning his marriage to Queen Victoria's grand-daughter, Victoria Eugenia, it was borne in on him that there was nowhere in town where a fellow could put up his wedding guests in the manner to which they, and he, were accustomed. Used to the best, he called in the great César Ritz and his *beaux arts* architect Charles Mewès, whose work, modelled on their Paris masterpiece, he admired on visits to the London Ritz.

Neither the king nor the master hotelier thought small. They went for lofty, vaulted ceilings and room-to-room vistas and decorated them in cream and white for added airiness. And in case the effect of this might be a touch austere, they covered every inch of floor with made-to-measure carpets woven at the royal factory. Each one – a different design for every room – is signed and dated.

Like perhaps no other hotel, the Ritz is central to the life of the city it adorns, partly because, thanks to its origins and present associations, it is the semi-official residence for visiting royalty and heads of state. Guests have included the honeymooning Rainiers, the Prince of Wales, Henry Kissinger, Paloma Picasso and the Windsors, who had their special suite-with-a-view. It is also the hub of Madrid social life quite simply because it is the best place to be for almost anything you have in mind. When the Ritz gives its annual New Year's Eve bash in the great *salon real*, or its June reception to celebrate the opening of the garden, all Madrid, the women *soignées*, the men patricians, will be there, because that is what one does.

As you enter the place and feel your Lobb's sink into the hall carpet (replaced in 1981, at a cost of £300 a square yard, as part of the overall freshener) your first impression is that you are not in a hotel at all. There appears to be no reception area: reception is hidden in a room to your left, and manned by dignitaries sporting tails and red carnations. The porters' desk to your right is a simple, free-standing table. You advance into the vastness of the upper hall, where you can take your aperitif, or tea – for which the Ritz is as famous here as its London counterpart – or breakfast on fresh salmon and champagne. You will find no bar, nor see a bottle until it is wafted to your table: like Claridges, they have felt no need for one, but the daring idea has recently been mooted.

To your right, for more solid sustenance, is the restaurant, but it is more than just a pretty place: this is haute cuisine at its hautest. The

Spanish chef – try his cream of melon with almonds – works with a French wizard, trained by the Haeberlin brothers, Bocuse and Lenôtre, which gives him at last count an eight-star background. Go for the salad of scallops and shrimps with piquant vinaigrette and fresh mint, or the tiny crêpes, also with shrimp, in a tomato and basil sauce: for a deeply inland city, Madrid is impressively big on fresh fish and seafood. As well as fish, there is fowl: pinky breast of duck with an onion marmalade. There is offal: calves' liver sautéed with honey vinegar and thyme. Meat, with a gesture to Californian surf 'n' turf: a medallion of veal with prawns in a curry sauce. Or there is game – in season, you may down a plump partridge previously downed by the top guns of a private shoot on the estate of the Duke of Fernán Núñez, no less.

All this, of course, however local the origins of the ingredients, has a distinctly French, not to say 'international', flavour, and the new General Manager, a fervent patriot, is eager to see some changes made. Madrilenes who frequent his hotel – and it is suggestive that the word 'Ritz' comes out as 'rich' in the local pronunciation – and are looking for French haute cuisine can, and do, jet off to Paris for the odd dinner. Toque-hunting is on for a top Spanish chef – probably Catalan or Basque – to partner the talented Buret and introduce some classic Spanish dishes to the repertoire.

Another, more revolutionary project: plans are afoot to open up the restaurant to the street (permission being granted, for the Ritz is classified as a national monument), thus integrating the hotel even further into the life of the city of which it is already an important hub.

Through the restaurant is the terrace – step carefully over the outstretched boots of polo players relaxing after a game – and, beyond that, below the balustrade, the garden. In spring and summer you lunch and dine here on simple fare, say a club sandwich, under azure parasols in a semi-tropical oasis, the rumble of workaday traffic screened by the surrounding shrubbery. Serious eating happens on the terrace, and serious drinking, too – from the prodigious cellar you might try the Waltraud Torres or the Imperial Cune, both 1978 for preference.

At the bottom of the garden, to the left, is the street entrance and through it, hey presto, the Prado. So when you have viewed the

Velásquez and gazed at the Goyas, you can nip over to the Ritz for some less spiritual refreshment.

A slightly shorter version appeared in *The Times* (16 June 1990)

WINES FROM SPAIN

ANDREW HENDERSON

I never travelled to Spain with Ray. I went with him to Italy: he to receive, from the House of Bolla, the Bologna trophy for his book *The Wines of Italy*; me, I now like to think, under his tutelage to learn the art of travelling in the world of wine. He could demonstrate that art like few others. Not for him the boring discomfort of bottling line inspections, nor the irrelevant tasting in a damp cellar of young, undrinkable wines, sucked up by pipette out of their wooden cask, tannic, unfiltered and mouth-puckeringly unpleasant. Wines were for drinking in appropriate surroundings, with food, in good company and, if joined by ladies, preferably at their tantalizing attractive best. Whether with dons in dining roms or alfresco by a meadow in a punt, wine was a part of the fun of life. Little did I realize, as we flew by private jet to land at the military airport near Verona, that I would rarely travel again in such company and comfort. What a way to start: what a teacher.

I regret not visiting Spain with Ray. There is so much to see, enjoy and learn, from some of the kindest people, the sort who have that innocent confidence which reveals pride as they present their region, their culture, their food and wine. And the pleasures of Spain expanded to new dimensions in the Olympic year of 1992, the wines gaining greater recognition, some outstripping northern neighbours on quality, and many more winning with value for money.

No Spaniard could have awarded prizes for books when Ray received his, for there were no books of merit on Spanish wines, except for sherry. Even *Imbiber* readers have to search hard through the collection for references to Spain. The brilliant piece on sherry and its birthplace in *Imbiber 3* by John D. Stewart is as fresh as fino, but even a Victorian classic of 1865 by Robert Druitt, a Medical Officer of Health, under the comprehensive title *Report on the Cheap Wines from France, Italy, Austria, Greece, and Hungary: their Quality, Wholesomeness and Price* (and a further 20 words) still does not mention Spain. John Reay-Smith wrote one of the first books on the subject in 1974, *Discovering Spanish Wine*, and modest as these early books now seem they were at the time rays of brilliant light. Jan Read with Maite Manjon, Tony Lord and Kathryn McWhirter with Charles Metcalfe and Hubrecht Duijker have now given erudite detail and confirmation of the giant leaps that Spanish wines are making.

Spain has always been the largest European vineyard, with a greater variety of vines than many suspect, but it has never been the biggest producer. This is due to the size and layout of the country and its various climates; but it has taken time for those outside to learn of the treasures within. Winston Churchill, casting his vote "to this unknown claret", stumbled upon Vega Sicilia, the classic from Ribera del Duero. The Marqués de Riscal and Marqués de Murrieta acquired fame as producers of the best wines from Rioja, and Miguel Torres Carbó made determined thrusts to export his Catalan wines. Unknowingly some, sipping the sacrament at the altar, drank wine from Tarragona; but few knew what Spain offered. Saffron and olives were as well known as flamenco and paella, and all more so than wine.

Today, after nearly two decades of national investment through their London Commercial Office under the banner Wines from Spain, wines displaying the individual styles and regional differences are being recognized and enjoyed. Controlled by a Consejo Regulador de la Denominación de Origen (DO) these emergent regions are changing the image and opportunities for Spanish wines. There are now 39 DOs in Spain, forming a well-regulated and improving base for a modern industry, and with the many new roads now built, it is relatively easy to travel into wine regions and witness the changes, meet the people and absorb the wonders of this country.

You could begin in Galicia. Near the western promontory of Cabo de Finisterre are three DOs – Ribeiro, Valdeorras and, closest to the Atlantic, Rías Baixas, making the best of the white wines based on the Albariño grape: crisp, lightly *pétillant* and nearly thirst-quenching. Some consider Albariño to be potentially the best of Spanish whites, although those who adore the wood-aged classics from Cataluña or Rioja will only ever be admirers, not converts. Old-fashioned signs for 'ostras y Albariño' remind us of the never far-off sea, as do the scallop shell shields, immediately recognizable to a never-ending flow of pilgrims to Santiago de Compostela as the shield of St James, reputedly buried there. The magnificent twin-towered baroque cathedral justifies any visit, but take time to gaze at the stunning neo-classical Palacio Rajoy.

Tourists in Galicia find Amandi the recommended red wine, but the best often seems in short supply. Should you ever be attracted by 'Queimada', Spain's interpretation of *aguardiente* or *marc*, heed a local tip: wear a lapel badge, legibly displaying a name you'll admit to, with a local address.

Travelling inland, a visit to Salamanca is rewarding simply to admire Spain's finest *plaza mayor*. Built by Alberto Churriguera between 1729 and 1755, its harmony and beauty inspire tourist and student alike and remind us again of the country's architectural wealth. And from here you can drive north to visit three DOs.

Ribera del Duero has a turreted Hollywood-style castle straddling the hilltop of Peñafiel, under which the cooperative produces typical red wines. When awarded DO status in 1982 the region's only wine of international repute was Vega Sicilia but now Viña Pesquera has an enviable following, too. Using Tinto Fino, Garnacha and a touch of the white Albillo grape, the owner Alejandro Fernández macerates on skins for over three weeks, and gives his wines two years in French and American oak. The combination of good skin contact and oak-ageing results in a wine which some regard as typical, others as individualistic, but American journalists have attributed to it qualities which made it a star overnight. The DO has no white wines.

Move on to Rueda, a classic example of developments in Spain, and you certainly find whites. Situated on a deceptively high plateau

which creates advantageous temperature variations, it attracted the
Marqués de Riscal firm to produce crisp fresh wines in their Vinos
Biancos de Castilla winery in 1974, six years before DO status was
conferred, and a few years after Miguel A. Torres had produced the
first of Spain's whites in temperature-controlled stainless steel. Ris-
cal now produce a range of stylish modern whites, using the classic
Verdejo grape, deftly aged in oak, as well as the noble Sauvignon
Blanc and the Viura, a variety with which they were familiar, but
never totally satisfied, in Rioja. (Rueda DO wines must contain 25
percent Verdejo. With 60 percent Verdejo they become Rueda
Superior, such as the Marqués de Griñon wines made for him by
Antonio Sanz in his Bodegas de Castilla la Vieja.)

Rueda's other claim to fame is the Estación Enológica, one of the
best-equipped wine laboratories in Europe. Its job is to support,
control, discipline and experiment. Carrying out over 20,000 ana-
lytical tests a year, half of which are checks on quality or elimination
of any fraud, those trained here achieve in a morning what was a
month's work five years ago.

The third of the DOs to visit is Toro in the province of Zamora.
Zamoran reds, the traditional wines of the dons of Salamanca's university, can be as thick as soup, but the best made from Tempranillo
and usually labelled (legally) as Tinto de Toro, are genuinely
balanced, full-bodied wines showing attractive fruit with modern
oak ageing. Bodegas Fariña with their Gran Colegiata set standards,
achieving somewhat lower, and authorized, alcohol levels than their
forebears.

South to the capital the new DO Vinos de Madrid produces red,
white and *rosado* wines. Its vineyards cover three defined sub-
regions and in one, just off the main road south to Valdepeñas, the
small non-wine town of Chinchón is famous for its *anis* and a welcoming Parador. South again, and west of Toledo, is the source of
the Marqués de Griñón red wine originally recommended by the late
Alexis Lichine, a towering man of the wine world: a little overrated
for some tastes, but it has caused a buzz in a number of markets.

In DOs of central Spain, Méntrida, La Mancha (the Don Quixote
DO) and, further south, Valdepeñas, all produce sound wines which
without being particularly memorable often offer good value and
have put the whole area firmly on the wine map.

East on the Mediterranean coast, inland from Alicante and Valencia, a clutch of DOs in Levante have large-scale *bodegas* with the common denominator of technology combined with eager entrepreneurial activity. Cajoled by overseas buyers and an awareness of EC opportunities these regions have transformed their wines for export to supermarket shelves.

Uniquely there is an event in Valencia, awesome in scale, though unconnected with wine. At midnight on the final day of the Fallas de San José, a year's work goes up in smoke. Originating from a pagan festival, brotherhoods work the year round in hangars creating ten- to thirty-foot *papier mâché* effigies or *fallas*, impressive in detail and colour, depicting dramatic themes: political, historical and allegorical. Only the winning *falla*, judged by local dignitaries, escapes the bonfire of all bonfires. A breathtaking festival symbolizing the impermanence of material and physical being.

Back north to Rioja. Rioja has a permanence. It is surrounded by mountains above coloured and patterned plains of fields and meadows, cut by rivers and tree lines and distorted by random remnants of castle-topped rocks. This is a part of Hemingway's Spain. The winemaking sub-regions Rioja Alta, Alavesa and Baja mostly display a traditional scene of low bushy vines of the authorized grapes: Tempranillo, Garnacha, Graziano and Mazuelo are the red varieties with Viura the predominant white. Traditional blending and ageing too make their subtle contribution to the different wine styles. The more famous reds are '*crianza*' (aged in oak). 'Vino de Crianza' on a back label issued by the Consejo Regulador indicates a wine held in wood for a year to give some of that soft round character, making it an easy drinking wine. '*Reserva*' confirms three years' ageing in wood and bottle, and '*Gran Reservas*', the wines that have shattered foreign reputations, have a minimum of two full years in wood and a further three in wood or bottle. The skill of the winemakers is in selecting the appropriate method and timing, reflecting traditions, style and quality of each *bodega*, and what they judge to be best for a particular vintage.

Visits to Rioja are fun but no wine routes lead logically past names familiar from labels. Logroño, the regional capital, is undoubtedly the international centre of car horn hooting, but no wine museum or monument forms the focal point. Simply, it is modern, busy and wealthy: the town where most people stay. The wine capital is Haro, now brought closer by a new direct road, but once inside its streets you are lost in time: the timelessness that is the essence of Rioja. Even a welcome new hotel, opened in November 1989, has been there forever, variously as a monastery, hospital barracks and prison. Nothing really changes. Definitely not The Tertre restaurant with its trellised tables and benches, the deep baker's oven for the lamb and kid specialities of the region, relished by the locals enjoying the local vino out of plain bottles – with no back labels. No costly ageing for the locals' pleasure, though classic Riojas can be had. This is a place entirely unpretentious and authentic.

The 1850s saw Bordeaux vineyards afflicted by oidium, a mildew which destroys healthy grapes. The French, compelled to find new wine supplies, turned to their close neighbour, Rioja. But in the late 1860s a second, far more devastating, problem began destroying European viticulture. *Phylloxera vastatrix*, a vine pest which attacks European vine roots but American vine leaves, started its remorseless invasion of Bordeaux vineyards. During the next decade many properties were utterly ruined, forcing a migration of *vignerons* with expertise and talents to Rioja, where they capitalized on the region's ancient industry.

Many now-familiar Rioja names were established at this time. Marqués de Riscal, the first (but now usually bracketed with Marqués de Murrieta), Tondonia, Berberana, CUNE, Riojanas and Paternina among them. But phylloxera, which contemporary *vignerons* believe will survive even a nuclear war, was still to overrun Spain. The solution was to graft European varieties onto resistant American rootstock, but the scourge was nonetheless a major setback and progress slowed everywhere.

In 1926 Rioja set up the DO legislation, making later additions to it, and occasionally new *bodegas*, Muga among them, were established; but in wine terms nothing dramatic occurred until 1970. Then wine prices soared in Bordeaux, sending frantic British merchants to look everywhere. They fell upon a jewel. Unchanged for over a century Rioja's stock of fine aged wine was available, underpriced and ready to be plundered. Export successes attracted investment and new names appeared. Marqués de Cáceres was established by the owners of Château de Camensac in Bordeaux.

Olarra, in a revolutionary modern *bodega*, set out to combine tradition with technology. The sherry house of Domecq planted the biggest vineyard in the region's history, created by negotiating for 1,062 different individual vineyards in order to establish a modern layout manageable by the same methods used in Jerez. By contrast, Contino is a small artisanal single-vineyard wine, but one of the prettiest and finest in Rioja.

Closer to the Pyrenees, Pamplona's San Fermin festival with the running of the bulls (one of Hemingway's passions) and the deliciously drinkable *rosado* wines sum it up for many when they think of Navarra, Rioja's neighbouring DO region. But the viticultural station, EVENA, influences the progress of Navarra and no other DO shows greater optimism as it moves through the 1990s. Similarly, the oenological station of Movera in Aragón helps a group of DOs to modernize and in Somontano, a new DO since 1987, just south of the central Pyrenees, there is work with a range of local and noble European varietals. There are high hopes for Somontano.

The region most associated with imported European varietals is the Penedès DO in Cataluña, the northeast triangle of Spain, hemmed in by the Pyrenees to the north and the Mediterranean to the south. The *bodega* in the vanguard of the development was Torres. During and after his studies at Dijon and inspired by his work with noble European varietals, Miguel A. Torres persuaded his father to introduce changes on the family estate. He set up a controlled experimental programme using a range of clones for new white and red varietals, planting plots of vines in different parts of the estate. Virtually across the road, in Plà del Penedès, Jean León, originally from Santander but living in California, had bought a vineyard. Knowing how much French wines appealed to Californians he planted Cabernet Sauvignon and Chardonnay throughout his estate. The contrasting approaches of these two estates gave ample proof of the suitability of the Penedès for viticultural development with noble varietals, but it was over a decade before others followed the lead.

Simultaneously, in the original Torres winery, work began with stainless steel and temperature control for the fermentation of both traditional and experimental wines, and wood-ageing experiments were under way for the increased range of reds. All of this, under the careful supervision of Miguel A. Torres, has been the foundation for the rapid development of Torres wines since the 1960s. Acknowledged by many as Spain's greatest winemaker, Torres' astonishing output continues. In terms of energy and determination he followed a tireless parental example. But by lecturing, writing books in a number of languages, and working on his estates in three continents across two hemispheres he broke new ground. In the early 1980s Miguel A. Torres took a sabbatical at Montpellier to find answers to many of the viticultural problems he felt would be the challenges of the '90s. Inspired, he allowed no let-up in the pace of development and has capitalized on the range of microclimates throughout the estate. Four wines, now designated as his *pago* (small plot) wines, come from selected family vineyard sites. These were chosen, following some twenty years of observation, when a specific varietal demonstrated excellent compatibility with altitude, site, soil and microclimate in that particular vineyard: Mas La Plana (Cabernet Sauvignon), Mas Borras (Pinot Noir), Milmanda (Chardonnay) and Castell de Fransola (Parellada and Sauvignon Blanc).

This development could only have occurred in the Penedès because of the range of microclimates at contrasting altitudes. Relevant results and changes in any aspect of viticulture and winemaking are compared with activity on the Torres Chilean estate, and each can learn from the other. Similarly, the latest vineyard in Sonoma, California, where Marimar Torres watches over all activities, both contributes and benefits. Given the range of microclimates in the Penedès, which allows successful cultivation of the different varietals; the size and the discipline in the Torres winery which handles one of the longest harvests; and the intellectual stimulation, there is probably no other winery in Europe where you will learn as much in a week. The Miguel Torres Wine Course, run for their international customers, provides enjoyable proof for that thought.

Throughout the 1960s and '70s many Spanish aficionados dreamt of the current success of the Wines from Spain campaign. To honour the efforts of bureaucrats, marketing people, restaurateurs, wine writers, merchants and makers – of people who, as the citation goes, have shown exceptional endeavour in promoting Spain's quality wines – the Gran Orden de Caballeros del Vino was founded in London in 1984. Unique in being the only national order or wine fraternity, the roll call to date totals twenty-three and includes, among the earliest, Hugh Johnson, to the most recent, Allan Cheesman of Sainsbury's, with Miguel A. Torres the first winemaker to be honoured.

Much as this reflects quality and endeavour, we also find now, on a hard-nosed commercial level, that there is sufficient development and variety for a trade fair to be held in London on alternate years dedicated solely to Wines from Spain. Mind you, I don't think Ray cared for trade fairs.

"COME TO THE COOKHOUSE DOOR, BOYS"

PETER LUKE

British soldiers in the Peninsula had, it seemed, a savage, sullen and relentless appetite for beef. It was almost a case of "no beef, no war". The fact that the Government was seldom up to date with pay mattered little beside the troops' devouring passion for beef. In consequence, and owing to the hopeless inadequacies of the commissariat, they were not infrequently close to starvation. Their Spanish allies, more particularly the irregulars (*guerrilleros*), often fared much better.

General Sir Harry Smith, a subaltern in the 95th Rifles at the outbreak of war in 1808, first met the guerrilla leader, Julián Sanchez, while on reconnaissance after Wellington's breakout from the lines of Torres Vedras. Exploring the banks of the Coa river south-west of Salamanca, Harry was intercepted by a band of partisans and invited to attend upon their chief. Led up into the Sierra de Gata, from which the guerrillas made their frequent excursions to harrass the French lines of communication, he was eventually delivered to their headquarters, which he describes as follows:

> "Instead of a scene of debauchery and squalor, I saw a camp that would have done credit to a British cavalry regiment. Under the trees were properly laid out horse-lines and, at them, were men at 'stables' grooming their mounts in a thorough and diligent fashion. Beyond, under some umbrella-pines, were a number of *chozas* – huts made of cane and roofed with chestnut branches. A little way off to the right was a cookhouse area where a few men were busy tending charcoal fires and cutting vegetables into large earthenware casseroles. From these ascended a delicious aroma of charcoal smoke, stewing meat, and mountain herbs. Nearby there was even a mud bread-oven that had obviously been in use that very morning.
>
> "Everywhere in the camp there was activity. Behind the horse-lines two farriers worked at an anvil, and near them stood a number of horses, slack-hocked, waiting to be shod. Those not occupied with horses were cleaning flint-locks, sorting ammunition, mending saddles or spoke-shaving staves for *garrochas*.* Elsewhere a few men, those who had been relieved from sentry-go presumably, or had come off patrol, were wandering about picking snails off thistles for a purpose which I was soon to discover."

Harry is then introduced to their chief, Don Julián Sanchez.

> "The man I was confronted with was an even greater surprise than his camp. But for his black *charro*** costume I would have thought him an officer of the Rifles, so English did he look. So much so, in fact, that throughout the evening I kept seeing his face in the context of our Mess at Shorncliffe rather than in the mountain fastness of Extremadura."

---

* long lances used for herding bulls and, latterly, for poking at Frenchmen.
** horsemen of the province of Salamanca.

Harry, whose gastric juices had already been stimulated by the smells emanating from the camp-kitchen, was now happy to be invited to dine. To this end Sanchez led the way into a *choza* where a simple table was being laid by a villainous, bearded giant with a huge knife in his belt. This man, who answered to the name of '*El Fraile*' (the Friar) now took out his knife and, opening it with a series of alarming clicks, proceeded to draw the huge blade across a wholemeal loaf of bread which he hugged to his chest. At this moment another henchman entered with a steaming bowl of snails gleaming in a rich brown gravy, giving out a fragrance of garlic and wild fennel. Wishing the diners sustenance from the repast, the scullion withdrew and Harry was about to seat himself down when he observed *El Fraile* making a gesture which, being unused to Catholic ways, he adduced to be a blessing of the snails. Then all sat down and fell to.

In a long letter to his mother Harry describes the meal which followed.

> "In the regiment we had frequently mocked the French who eat with gusto such things as frogs and snails. Now the laugh was at my expense. I should mention that the snails here are different in appearance from those which you so diligently remove from your iris bed at home, the shells being in brown and yellow stripes like the coat of a tabby cat. But I have to admit that, once extracted from their carapaces – not always easy – they were tasty, though their preparation, so my hosts told me, was somewhat laborious since first they must be purged of their earthly droppings.
>
> "We had scarcely despatched the last of these succulent gastropods when the servant reappeared with a large earthenware casserole which he called an *olla podrida*. This, being construed, means 'putrid pot', which of course is the Spanish idea of a joke because the contents of this aromatic dish were anything but impure. Of a rich reddish colour, the stew – for that is what it was – had a basis of lentils and chick-peas in which were embedded morsels of tender kid together with slices of spicy sausage, peppers sweet and peppers hot, further flavoured with bay and other herbs of the mountainside.

"To accompany the stew came a dish of some green vegetable, dressed with oil and vinegar, which I was quite unable to
identify. On making enquiry (an informality which I thought
was allowable under the circumstances) I was informed that
the local thistle served a double purpose: not only did it nour-
ish the snails which we had already consumed, but the stalks,
stripped of their outer fibres and lightly boiled, can be eaten in
a variety of delicious ways.

"All in all good local produce was obviously the Order of the
Day, and more power to the *guerrilleros*. Would that our
Cockney riflemen could be persuaded to eat such wholesome
fare. Were they to do so, they would soon see off Monsieur
Frog – or should I say Snail? – in double-quick time. Needless
to say, by the time the three of us had got outside this substantial meal and sunk a two-litre jug of good red wine, I was
quite ready for bed – bed on this occasion, as on so many
others, being the herb-scented ground beside the camp-fire."

.   .   .

The friendship struck up between Harry Smith and Julián Sanchez in
the Sierra de Gata, stood the former in good stead on a subsequent
occasion – his marriage to Juana Maria De Los Dolores de León.
Juanita, as she was familiarly known, came from a good family in
Badajoz. She was just 14 when Lord Wellington decided – rightly as
events proved – that by prizing Soult's knuckles off that border fortress town, the war would open up and force the French finally to
loose their grip on the whole Peninsula. The full story of Juanita De
Los Dolores and Harry Smith is told elsewhere.* Here we are only
concerned with one brief aspect of it: their wedding breakfast.

Confronted with a pretty and recently orphaned 14-year-old who
had just escaped rape by drink-maddened British soldiery after the
storming of the town, Harry decided that the only effective form of
protection for Juanita was marriage to a British officer. He further
decided that he was the man for the job. Admirable as were his in-
tentions with the adrenalin still battle-high in his veins, he had no
doubt that all difficulties to this purpose could be overcome; just as

---

*Peter Luke, *The Other Side of the Hill*, London, 1984.

the regiment had, against all odds, overcome the fortress. He had had no time to calculate the new odds against him. In the first place Juanita was a Catholic and Harry, though a practising Christian, was not. Secondly, the only priest to be found in Badajoz had, very sensibly, locked himself into the crypt of the cathedral with all the church valuables and refused to come out. Harry, ever resourceful, suggested that perhaps for the occasion of a nuptial ceremony the priest might let him and Juanita in. The priest replied that this would be pointless since he could not perform a 'mixed marriage' without permission from the Bishop who was, wisely enough, eighty or so miles away in the Monastery of Guadalupe.

Harry, frustrated now and getting tired (he had not slept since the night before the battle), went to see his colonel, a kindly man called Andrew Barnard. Barnard, *in loco parentis*, as it were, warned Harry against the dangers of precipitate, foreign, and/or mixed marriages, but once having met the enchanting Juanita, he immediately offered to give away the bride. More, he said, he could not do.

Juanita now remembered having met in her own house a young priest who had called to see Lord Fitzroy Somerset and Captain Alexander Gordon, aides-de-camp to Lord Wellington, when they had been billeted on the De Los Dolores family two years previously. Harry therefore spurred himself – or rather his horse – on to Army Headquarters to find Gordon, who was by way of being a friend. Gordon, somewhat mystified by Harry's motives, nevertheless referred Harry to a nearby wayside inn where a detachment of guerrillas under Julián Sanchez were quartered.

This was the point when Harry, in the extremity of fatigue after recent events, might have felt like chucking in the sponge. But he had suffered a *coup de foudre* over the little Extremeña and love knows no bounds.

Sanchez received his Rifle Brigade acquaintance with great cordiality but their reunion was nearly spoilt by the guerrilla's excessive mirth at Harry's request for the priest, Father Julián.

"But," said Sanchez, "Padre Julián does not exist – for I was he. What, my friend, do you want a priest for anyway? You don't look like a Catholic."

When Harry explained that he intended to marry Juanita, Don Julián was at the same time delighted and astonished. Pointing across the bar-room to the ursine figure of 'El Fraile', he said, "There's your man. 'El Fraile' is not his nick-name. He's ninety-nine per cent Dominican Friar and one per cent *guerrillero*."

Harry, bemused by tiredness, looked doubtful. "Hombre, don't you understand? He's a priest. That's the man who will marry you."

And so it turned out to be. Within another forty-eight hours, during which time Harry had managed to get some sleep, he and Juanita were married, Colonel Barnard having given away the bride, and Harry's brother, Tom, who had pitched up that very day, having returned from hospital newly recovered from a wound, acting as best man. 'El Fraile' who always kept a stole in his saddle-bag against a priestly emergency (such as administering the Last Sacraments), conducted as near as he could get to a nuptial Mass (Harry being a Protestant) with great dignity. Julián Sanchez, with the collaboration of the innkeeper and his wife and daughters, provided the wedding breakfast to which nearly a hundred people sat down. Considering it was wartime the menu was little short of miraculous. But Spaniards like to rise to an occasion, and the occasion – an Anglo-Spanish marriage after the recapture of Badajoz from the hated and anti-Christian French – was worth rising to.

Unlike the French, who are masters of the planned cuisine, the Spanish are perfectly indifferent to the order in which dishes appear – so long as they are good and keep coming. On this day Harry and Juanita and their guests were regaled with *bacalao al Pil-Pil* – small pieces of dried salt cod, pre-soaked, then dropped into smoking hot olive oil with garlic and chillies. There was smoked ham of the sort known as *jamon serrano*, made from the half-wild, black-skinned, hairy Iberian pig which lives off acorns and snails and roots in the cork forests. A good shot by a *charro* had brought down a wild boar, first cousin to the Iberian pig. It arrived roasted whole, with a lemon in its mouth. Its flesh was pink, marbled with white fat.

Culinary activity was intense as the innkeeper and his daughters, amiably glistening with sweat, rushed in and out with ancillary dishes, expedited by shrill exhortations from Mama in the kitchen. There were *chorizos* – red spicy sausages; *butifarras* – a wide intestine filled with chopped meat mixed with pine-kernels, almonds and cinnamon; and *morcilla* – black pudding with onions and herbs. There were boiled potatoes in *all-i-olli*, artichoke hearts dressed with olive oil and lemon juice, red and green pimientos stuffed with rice and fried offal. There was tripe and pig's cheek with saffron and hot peppers: there were quails in white wine, and duck roasted with black olives. And finally, to crown the feast, there were *lechazos* – larded baby lambs stewed in wine from Almendralejo and garnished with mountain herbs. With all, served in large pitchers, was wine from Medallín and Zafra, red and white, rough and ready, and very strong.

And so began the married life of the Harry Smiths, which lasted many happy years until Harry, having survived so many campaigns, died of natural causes in 1860.

There is a chapel in St Mary's Church, Whittlesey, dedicated to the memory of Sir Harry Smith. In South Africa a town, Harrismith, in the Orange Free State, still bears his name. But, by chance, it was for Juanita to be given the greater memorial. When during the Boer War, in February 1900, a small dorp in Natal called Ladysmith was relieved after gallantly resisting a four-month siege half the world came to know of it. How many people, though, knew that Lady-smith had been named after a Spanish girl called Juanita who herself lived through two memorable sieges of her own home town, Badajoz?

I eat my peas with honey
I've done so all my life
I know you think it funny
But it keeps them on the knife . . .

ANON

When the duck and green peas came, we looked at each other in dismay; we had only two-pronged black-handled forks. It is true the steel was as bright as silver; but what were we to do? Miss Matty picked up her peas, one by one, on the point of her prongs . . . Miss Pole sighed over her delicate young peas as she left them on the side of her plate untasted, for they *would* drop between the prongs. I looked at my host: the peas were going wholesale into his capacious mouth, shovelled up by his large round-ended knife. I saw, I imitated, I survived!

MRS. GASKELL, Cranford (1853)

A FATHER IN WINE

KATHARINE WHITEHORN

When I shared an office with Cyril Ray on the *Spectator* for a couple of years in the early sixties, I knew nothing about wine at all – a delightful state to be in, because Ray took it upon himself to teach me.

It was easy to ask his advice. I remember once asking him what wine to buy to go with a particular occasion; I said I could go to six shillings. He listened carefully to what we were due to eat, and who was coming, and then said he thought a Perequita at five and ninepence would be just the thing. He would never talk you up into grandeur if it wasn't necessary.

He taught me why you don't pronounce the 't' in Montrachet, but why you do in Moët (the original Moot was a Dutchman). He explained about the classification of clarets to such good effect that when, a few years later, I had my first baby, its appearance was induced not by the tubes and drugs scheduled for me, but by a superb 1953 Gruaud Larose consumed the evening before. But the best introduction he ever gave me was in the matter of sweet white wines. I had just about reached the stage where I knew you shouldn't drink Château Yquem with steak, and said something jejune and disparaging about sweet wines. Ray was shocked, and set to work to convince me that they were superb in their own right, drunk with the correct food. He took me to marvellous tastings and lunches at places like Hallgarten in the City. There was no possibility of doing any work after such occasions.

It was around this time that the Rays produced Jonathan, now of Berry Bros. He had the unfortunate habit of doing his nightly yelling routine not between six and ten, like most babies, but after ten in the evening; this wore the Rays' nerves to a ravelling. Liz, in despair, asked the clinic what to do: the somewhat prim nurse said, with an air of great daring, "My dear – do you perhaps – er – have any – ahem – *sherry* in the house?" Liz allowed that perhaps they did, but Ray said no, "fortified wine's not good for little stomachs". The baby was soothed in the end by Israeli Sauternes.

The one drawback about sharing an office with Ray – I do not count our food rows as a drawback, they were immensely exhilirating – was the difficulty of actually doing any work; this tended to be done in the evenings instead. In the end, we were all leaving the *Spectator*, and I was already fashion editor of the *Observer*, and keen to continue to share an office with Ray. The solution: Ray joined the *Observer*, though obviously not just because I wanted him there. George Seddon, the man who appointed us both, insisted, however, that he be the one to break the glad news to me. He did so with a laconic memo: "Your other father figure joins the paper on July 9th." If you can have a father in law, and a father in God, can you have a father in wine? If so, Ray was certainly mine.

MEMORABLE
MEALS

NOT MUCH SILENCE
IN COURT: A STORY

ANTON CHEKHOV

Before going home to eat after a court sitting of the Justice of the Peace in N— village, the committee members retired to disrobe and to have a few minutes peace.

The Chairman of the committee, a stately man with bushy side-whiskers, who had to give his 'special opinion' on the recent proceedings, sat at the table and hurried to write it out.

The divisional representative of the village court was a young man with a dark melancholy face, named Milkin, reputed to be something of a philosopher, and dissatisfied with the average aims in life. He was standing at the window and gazing mournfully at the courtyard outside. The other more important divisional representatives had already departed. There remained a flabby, fat dignitary, who breathed heavily, and the assistant magistrate, a young German, who looked as if he suffered from catarrh, who was sitting on a small divan and waiting for the chairman to finish writing so that they could leave together to go to dinner.

In front of them stood the committee secretary, Zhilin, a little man with side-burns round his ears and with a sweet expression on his face.

He was talking in low tones and looking at the fat man with a honeyed smile.

"We're all longing to eat now because we are tired, and it's already four o'clock, but my dear Grigorii Savvich, it's not a real appetite. A real appetite, like a wolf's, comes only after physical exertion as it would when our ancestors returned from hunting with the hounds or after you've covered about a hundred versts* round your neighbourhood without stopping."

---

* *A verst* – 3500 English feet or 1.06 km

"Yes sir, much of it is in the imagination. Supposing let's say, you're on your way home with an appetite and looking forward to eating, then the mind doesn't enter into it; science and intellect always spoil the appetite. Where food is concerned philosophers and scientists are the bottom, and if I may say so the worst are the ones who don't even eat pork. When you're going home you have to try to keep your mind only on bottles and zakuski.* Once when I was on the road home I shut my eyes and conjured up a sucking pig with horseradish, which whetted my appetite so much that it brought on an attack of hysterics."

"Now sir, just when you come into your own courtyard there should be a smell of something good coming from the kitchen, you know what I mean . . ."

"Roast goose first and foremost," said the honourable member, sighing heavily.

"Grigorii Savvich, my dear fellow, you can't mean that. A duck is ten times better. The bouquet of goose hasn't the same tenderness and delicacy. You know the strongest is spring onions when they begin to brown, and if you get my meaning, to sizzle, the rogues, drifting over the whole house. Yes sir, when you enter the house the table must be laid, and you sit down, immediately tuck your napkin over your tie, stretch out a hand towards the vodka, taking your time. You don't pour it, our little mother vodka, into any old glass, but into some old-fashioned silver cup or some such round goblet; and don't drink it straight off, but first sniff it, rub your hands, look up at the ceiling nonchalantly, then, without hurrying, raise that little glass to your lips and straight away sparks travel from your stomach through your whole body . . . sparks."

The secretary's face had a blissful expression. "Sparks," he repeated, screwing up his face, "and the very minute you've drunk it you must take a bite."

"Listen," said the chairman, looking up at the secretary, – "a bit quieter! I've already ruined two pieces of paper on your account."

"Yes sir, I'm guilty, Pyotr Nikolaich. I'll be quiet," said the secretary and continued in a half whisper. "Now my dear Grigorii Savvich sir, you must also know how to set about the zakuski. You

* *zakuski* – hors d'oeuvres

have to know what to start with. The very best zakuski if you must
know, is the salted herring. Take a little bite with onion and mustard
sauce while you can still feel the fiery sparks; eat the caviar just as it
is, or if you like with a slice of lemon; after that a simple bit of radish
with salt; again the herring, but best of all kind sir, are yellow
capped saffron mushrooms, chopped finely like caviar, if you know
what I mean, with onion and olive oil – delicious! And burbot's liver
– that's a whole tragedy!"

"M-m, yes," agreed the honourable member, screwing up his
eyes, "fragrant white mushrooms."

"Yes, yes, yes! with onion, and you know with bay leaf and all
kinds of spices. When you open the pot and the steamy mushroom
smell rises, it sometimes even brings tears to your eyes. Now sir, the
minute the pie is out of the kitchen, then that very minute, as quick
as you can, you must take a second drink."

"Ivan Gur'ich," wailed the chairman plaintively, "I've ruined the
third page because of you."

"Devil take it – only thinking about eating," growled Milkin the
philosopher, showing his contempt. "Aren't there really more interesting things in life besides mushrooms or even fish pie?"

"Now sir, before you start the pie, take a drink," continued the
secretary in a low voice. You're already being carried away, like
when you hear a nightingale singing and hear nothing but its voice."

"The kulebyaka* must be appetising, shameless in all its naked-
ness, so that it's a temptation; your eye winks, and you cut out such a
big slice, holding it caressingly ... You start to eat it and butter
spurts out like tears, the stuffing is fat and juicy with giblets, eggs,
onion ..." The secretary rolled his eyes, his mouth stretching right
to his ears.

The honourable member wheezed and rubbed his hands, probably imagining a kulebyaka.

"The devil only knows," muttered the committee member, moving to the other window.

"Two slices have been eaten and the third is saved for the cabbage
soup," continued the secretary, sighing. "To keep your appetite
going, order the soup to be served as soon as you've finished the pie.

---

* kulebyaka – a pie

The soup must be burning hot; but best of all, my kind sir, borsh-chok from beets prepared the khokhlatskii manner with bacon and sausage, served with smetana* and fresh parsley and dill. Rassol'nik is also a splendid soup made from giblets and tender kidneys, and if you like soup then it's best made with root vegetables and herbs: carrots, asparagus, cauliflower and other judicious additions of a like nature."

"Yes, a splendid thing," sighed the chairman, tearing his eyes away from his paper, and immediately making a mistake, groaned.

"Show some respect. Otherwise I'll be writing the special opinion until nightfall. That's the fourth piece of paper ruined."

"I won't! I won't do it any more. I plead guilty, sir," the secretary excused himself and continued in a whisper: "as soon as you've supped the borshchok or the soup, order the fish course, kind sir. Of all the fish the best is roast carp with smetana, only you must put it promptly in milk the minute you get it, for twenty-four hours, to rid it of its muddy taste and to tenderize it.

"A sterlet is also very good," said the honourable member, closing his eyes; but to everyone's surprise, immediately heaved himself out of his seat, and looking furious, bellowed across to the chairman: "Pyotr Nikolaich, are you going to be quick? I can't wait any longer, I simply can't!"

"Let me just finish!"

"Alright then, so I'll go by myself! Devil take you!" The stout man waved his hands, seized his hat, and without saying goodbye, ran out of the room. The secretary sighed, and leaning down to the deputy magistrate's ear, continued in a low voice: "a pike or carp are also good with a tomato and mushroom sauce. But fish are not fill-ing, Stefan Frantsych; it's not a vital food; the main thing for a meal is not fish, not sauce, but the roast. Which sort of bird do you like best?"

The deputy magistrate made a sour face and sighed: "Alas, I have to draw the line at that: I suffer from stomach catarrh."

"No more of that sir, stomach catarrh is something the doctors have thought up; it's more an illness that comes from free thinking or from pride. Pay no attention to it. Let's suppose you don't want to

---

* *smetana* – soured cream

eat, or you're sick, and you ignore it and eat. If, suppose, they serve a couple of the greater snipe with the roast, surrounded by a little partridge or pair of plump quails – the females, then frankly you can forget about any catarrh. And a roast turkey? White, plump, and you know, juicy – rather like a nymph . . ."

"Yes, most likely it's tasty," said the deputy magistrate, smiling sadly. "I could eat turkey, if you like."

"But good heavens, a duck? If you take a young duck, caught when the first frosts come, and it's been roasted in a dish with potatoes, the potatoes finely cut and allowed to get golden and soak up all the duck fat, and that . . . "

The philosopher Milkin, with a wild look on his face, evidently wanted to say something, but suddenly smacked his lips, probably envisaging the roast duck; deprived of words, he seized his hat and hurriedly made off, drawn by invisible forces.

"Yes, maybe I could manage a little duck," sighed the deputy magistrate. The chairman stood up, said goodbye, and sat down again. "After the roast a man is satisfied and falls into a sweet stupor," continued the secretary. "Just at this moment your body feels good and you're in fine fettle. Just to finish off, for a dessert, you might manage three little glassfuls of spiced brandy." The chairman groaned, and crossed out an entire page. "I've spoilt the sixth page," he said angrily. "It's not conscientious work."

"Write, write, kind sir," began the secretary in a whisper. "I won't hinder. I'll be very quiet, I promise. Stefan Frantsych," he continued in a barely audible tone, "home-made spiced brandy is better than any champagne. After the first little glass the smell transports your whole soul – a kind of mirage; it seems to you that you're no longer sitting in your armchair at home but somewhere else in Australia on the softest ostrich . . ."

"Oh, very well, let's go Pyotr Nikolaich," said the deputy magistrate, shifting his legs restlessly.

"Yes sir," continued the secretary, "when you have your spiced brandy send up a few smoke rings from a good cigar, and then such dreamy thoughts will enter your head. You could be a generalissimo or married to the most beautiful woman in the world who swims all day before your eyes in some pool with golden fish. She swims, and you say to her: 'darling, come and kiss me!'"

"Pyotr Nikolaich," moaned the deputy magistrate.

"Yes sir," continued the secretary, "having had your smoke, pick up your dressing gown from the floor and off to bed. Lie on your back, stomach up, and take the newspaper. When your eyes are closing and you're on the borderland of dreams, it's pleasant to read about politics: let's see – they've blundered in Austria; there France has upset someone; there a catholic priest has gone against the rules – you read, and it's very pleasant."

The chairman jumped up, flung aside his pen, and seized his hat with both hands. The deputy magistrate, forgetting his catarrh and overcome with impatience, also jumped up. "Let's go," he cried.

"Pyotr Nikolaich, what about the special opinion?" said the secretary, aghast. "When will you be able to write it, my kind sir? You have to be in town at six o'clock you know."

The chairman threw up his hands and rushed towards the door. The deputy magistrate also waved his hands, and seizing his portfolio, disappeared with the chairman. The secretary sighed, cast a reproachful glance after them, and started to gather up the papers.

Translation of 'The Siren', extract from *Russian Food, All the Peoples, All the Republics* (1989)

If the soup had been as hot as the claret, the claret as old as the bird, and the bird had had the breast of the parlour-maid it would have been a damned good dinner . . .

ANON Quoted by Sir Harry Luke, *The Tenth Muse*

THE DAMASCUS PLUM

JANE GARDAM

The better the soil they say the uglier the country; but I've never found East Kent ugly and (so they also say) when you're in sight of Ash steeple you're standing on the richest earth in England – miles and miles of crumbly light-coloured silt that was once swum over by all the fishes in the cold North Sea. It looks lovely most of the year, ridged with thousands of blue cabbages and cream and green and smelly cauliflowers, purple with raddichio and, in high summer, again at last for it's been gone since 1939, some wonderful fields of sky-blue flax.

Inward from Deal and seaward along the peninsular from Canterbury are vast market gardens and kitchen gardens flanking the roads and rough hand-painted signs with curious spellings say 'Hay, walnuts, cobs'. In autumn trestle tables are piled up with corn cobs so cheap they're almost free. In winter there's the lovely black-and-white geometry of the hop gardens. You look through the cats'-cradle wires at the oasts and the sky. Lettuces in spring lie in acres along the edge of the golf course near the sea at Sandwich Bay, like petals resting before being blown away to Belgium: but a week later with sprinklers flinging themselves about above them they're sitting up straight and nicely rooted. There are good lettuces often just lying around for the picking up, like the cabbages that grow wild along the white cliffs of Dover. Stray cauliflowers after the harvest roll about in the ditches like heads after a revolution. Walking last year near lovely Paramour Farm I came on a good-sized hill of dumped gooseberries, waxy and gold like crystallised fruits and fizzing with wasps. Under the armies of manicured fruit trees were bright trickles and scatterings of apples the pickers had missed. Some of the trees had the traditional top apple left for luck. East Kent has a hard climate and hard-headed people but there's a feeling of abundance and even extravagance sometimes when it comes to fruit and veg.

Richness and ruthlessness. Apple orchards, pear orchards heart-

breakingly beautiful in spring you find suddenly gone, but almost
before you're done mourning you see other trees planted out to replace them. Apple crops may be rather fewer now but East Kent
people still know about them and you won't hear anyone in the
shops in Deal or Sandwich or round Fordwich asking for 'apples'
but for Discoveries or Greensleeves or John o' Golds. And potatoes
are never potatoes but nearly always Desirées.

Fish is pretty serious, too. In Deal there are five fish shops, at least
two with their own boat. There are fishermen's genes in Deal. The
pier is crowded with rods – from babes to octogenarians and people
in wheelchairs – and you even have to pay them at three o'clock in
the morning. I once saw three small boys on the prom dragging in
the direction of Griggs's in South Street something large and grey
and uncommonly like a dead mermaid: for opinion only, I'd guess. I
don't see Mr Griggs offering such a thing for sale.

There's no smell of fish in the East Kent fish shops, only of salt
water and the sea-side. You don't bother to go to any of the shops if
it's been very rough weather. A little frozen fish is kept, so I hear, but
it's out of sight and only offered to the tourists.

When the marble slabs are full, though, you see folk choosing
things you seldom see in London – huge packages of bright silver
sprats (twenty pence a pound), large whiskery things in shells and
great big sunset-coloured undressed crabs. Children up on shoulders
are given a twisted paper full of prawns instead of a Big Mac and the
other day there was a grimy old girl in after a black belligerent lobster: "It's for me friend. It's her birthday." It doesn't sound very
English does it? Well – that depends. Could it be perhaps an inter-
mingling of French blood from across the Straits? Just don't try
suggesting it.

The elite of East Kent makes its way to the Messrs Cavell, a tiny
fish shop between Walmer and Deal facing the sea. You stand in rev-
erent silence and politely rather far from the counter where one Mr
Cavell or another gives recommendations – and instructions about
cooking should you ask. There's never anything so common as a
queue at Cavell's and there is very little fish to be seen, though the
brothers smoke their own haddock and cod and used to pot their
own shrimps before the EEC. At intervals the Cavells will disappear
behind a screen to an inner sanctum, like Orthodox priests at the

holy part of the service, and little clinking noises of ice and sharp knives and rushing water can be heard. The fish are brought for inspection, taken back and operated on out of sight, returned for re-inspection, taken back again and at last emerge wrapped in quantities of fresh grease-proof to be exchanged for a large amount of money. To be invited to dinner by a good cook in reach of an East Kent fish shop is an invitation I'd prefer to almost any restaurant, anywhere.

Yet do they know this in the rest of Europe? No they do not as will be exemplified by the story of my one-time Swiss pupil Klaus whom I met first many years ago in Kent and then again in 1991 in his full majesty on the shores of Lac Léman above that discriminating city of veal and cream, Geneva.

I had been told of the boy Klaus by a woman I hardly knew who was a friend of Klaus's uncle and two aunts who lived together in a Kent village not far from Eyethorne. They had just adopted Klaus. His mother, the third sister, had died earlier in the year. She had been married to a Swiss who had died some years before and Klaus was their only child. The uncle and aunts were trying to get the boy into an English public school for which he had to pass the Common Entrance examination. "*Very* clever," the woman said, "*very* bright. English perfect but – well, I expect they'll explain. If they can. They're not very talkative themselves. They're Naval." "Naval?" I thought of oranges. I thought of birth. "He was R.N. and a sister was a Wren. They're mad on the land, like retired naval people are. None of them married – you know the sort of thing. It's not very usual nowadays. There's a difficulty with imagination, somewhere and the boy's half Swiss into the bargain. You do this sort of coaching don't you? I thought you did. They'll be ever so grateful."

The address took me over the flat countryside inland for a mile or so, through Shatterling and Ash and past haunted Bekesbourne, then through cornfields on the narrow field-lanes. It meant following signposts from one deserted cross-roads to the next. Klaus's village was up a narrow road that said it was a dead-end and stopped being metalled as it became the village street. The house – it was called Plum Cottage – was at the far end of this and looked out on either side and from the back at gardens, then fields and a river, sleeping elms and beeches and black, fat cows strolling along the river bank. The sky was huge. The small lovely village was deserted and asleep.

The boy himself came to the door and stood back holding the mock medieval latch. I could see right through the cottage – the passage was scattered with wellington boots and very little furniture – to the garden where a stalwart man was toiling in a rosebed. Over the cottage door, late roses were splayed out evenly over do-it-yourself-shop fans of trellis and had metal tags on them. Between the roses the boy Klaus stood spotty, bolshy, leathern-lidded, sullen-eyed, limp-handed and so sadly thin he looked concave. I thought he looked at me with distaste but then thought perhaps it was just misery.

Round the corner of the front of the house trudged an aunt pushing a wheel-barrow. We turned back to her and she set down the handles and, as we talked, took a hunk of bread out of her pocket and began to eat. Then, as the boy and I went into the house and passed the kitchen door a second aunt peeped out. The kitchen seemed full of chrysanthemum cuttings. On the table was one tin of soup, labelled 'family size', two small tins of baked beans and a loaf of sliced white bread. In the study where Klaus and I sat at a desk facing the window the uncle in the flowerbed stepped out of it and passed us by, making a sketchy naval salute but not looking at us. Later I noticed him standing beside a compost heap peeling a banana. He dropped the skin thoughtfully on the heap and then after a moment threw the banana in after it.

Klaus was clever all right, whatever clever means. He had a magnificent memory and was already a distinguished linguist, his English not only utterly confident but colloquial and idiomatic and quite accentless. He said that his French and German were about equal to it and his Italian was "coming along". Mathematical subjects he said had "never been any trouble" to him – and I believed him for I soon found that he had a formidable rational faculty.

But I was here to teach him how to write the compulsory imaginative essay paper and of this he had not the slightest notion. We went through several specimen papers, we read essays from Steele to V. S. Pritchett. I gave him all my notes, I asked him to describe things – anything: how he got up in the morning, how the earth went round the sun. Every essay title he greeted with a small derisive smile. "This one," he said pointing to last year's papers, "'Travelling'. It cannot be done. It is impossible. It is too precise for something so all encompassing."

"Then say so. Discuss it."

"That wouldn't be polite would it? And impolitic. It would antagonise them."

"Not at all. Or not necessarily. You're being too literal. Too serious. Just put down something – you know about travelling."

"I've only travelled once. By air here from Geneva and then by car from Gatwick airport."

"Well, that's more than a lot of people have done on this earth. And you can talk of travelling if it's just over the fields into Canterbury or just walking through the garden here down to the river. Sitting in this chair and thinking is a kind of travelling. Think of the – concept."

"But whoever would want to know all that?"

"Well, you'd have to make it interesting."

"But it doesn't make me interested."

"Well then—." It was another lesson later in the week. "Well then. What does interest you? Let's work from the other way round."

"Maths. And some translations. And—," his blank eyes looked far away and he stared out at the evening. His uncle and aunts were not on the scene tonight but a basket chair with a pale squashy cushion stood under some little trees beside a brick wall made of soft Kent reds. The uncle's hat lay on the grass and the colour in the flower bed was glowing and saddish as the day began to die. I remembered Klaus's mother had just died and he'd had no father for years.

"Well," I said, "Do what you can with it." He walked me, as usual, politely to the front door and past the kitchen where the second more female and landward aunt was burning some baked beans on a very old gas stove. "Oh dear," she called, "I'm afraid we're not great cooks here. The garden is too big for us." I saw for the first time in Klaus's eye a look of total incomprehension.

Over the next few weeks, as Klaus and I sat in tortured struggle to unlock one shred of his soul, the smell of burning or boiling-over food and the haphazard munching of his ambulant relations began to attack my nerves as well. Once as I heard his stomach give tongue I brought out some chocolate.

"Go on. Eat it."

Perhaps he had got past it all for he said, "Thank you but I only eat Swiss chocolate."

"Try this."

"No. What I should very much like would be a meal. At which people sit down together."

"I'll bring you some Swiss chocolate next time," I said, "and we'll eat it together. Look – describe to me what hunger is like."

He looked amazed once again. He was always looking amazed. "There's nothing much to say except of course that it is unpleasant."

"*Like*? Like *what*? Think of something it is *like*."

"This is what you've been saying – a metaphor?"

"Exactly. Use one. Make one."

"It feels—. Hunger is like itself. There is no comparable situation, I feel."

"Oh, for God's sake. Look—." (I would be rash. I would be cruel.) "Just describe something else then that's unpleasant. Describe death. Tell me about it."

"How can I. I have not died."

"Very well then. Tell me about your mother. Tell me about your mother's death."

"I was not present."

"Well, describe how the news was broken to you. Go on. Do it. Were you in the house at the time? In a hospital?"

"It was a clinic."

"Describe the clinic. What happened. *Now*. Go on. I'll go out of the room if you like."

"That's all right."

But I did go out and across the garden and walked to the three small damson trees. Their old trunks were covered with green-white fluffy bark. They felt rough on my fingers but warm from the sun. The blue-black fruits clustered in the pale leaves. Some spindly spiky branches were heaped near the trees where the uncle had been taking out dead wood. Nearby were bigger branches sawn into little logs, dense heavy queer old wood, old as the wall they stood against, and older. The branches smelled of damsons and old summers long forgotten. Oh how to reveal some of it to this dead boy.

He came dragging his big feet over the grass with his essay on death hanging from his hand. It read something like this.

> "At 13.40 my mother was in a plastic hood containing oxygen. It was fixed over the bed. She had a machine in her hand against her mouth. The hospital was very well-organised and effective and when a nurse told me that my mother was unable to hear me and had closed her eyes, making any communication between us impossible, I accepted what she said. The nurse suggested that I might like to go for a cup of coffee in her office at the end of the ward. This I did and at 13.50 heard some people hurrying along the corridor outside and I saw a doctor go by. At 13.59 the nurse came to inform me that my mother was dead."

"Klaus—. Well, Klaus—. Go back again. Look – in your head. *Suffer*, Klaus. *Remember*."

He sat down in the creaky chair and stared up into the plum trees. He wrote on the pad something like this.

> "They asked me almost at once (14.03) if I would like to take home my mother's wedding ring as it would only be taken otherwise by the funeral furnishers and perhaps lost. At 14.30 or thereabouts they brought it and her other belongings. At 14.35 I declined to see the body of my mother, saying that I wished to remember her as in life. I had heard that this is a thing that is said. They offered me more coffee and asked if there was someone at home I might like to telephone so that they could come to the clinic to fetch me, but I said no to both these suggestions. At 14.40 I left the hospital."

"Klaus—." (It was a courtroom statement.) "Oh, Klaus!"

"Listen," he said, "Listen, Anne—" (I had a moment's hope.)

"Anne, my mother wasn't a nice woman. I didn't like her. I didn't mind her dying."

"I give up."

We both stared up at the trees and the little plums looked down on us and the bark shone pink and silver in the evening sun.

"What sort of a plum is it?"

"It's a damson. It's very tasty. We love it. It's a very old plum and it's been here for hundreds of years. It's called the Damascus plum. St Paul must have eaten it."

"Does it taste good?"

"Very good when it's cooked. It's sharp. It's what's called a strong plum and it needs sugar. Wonderful with cream. The two colours together look—."

"I've never tasted a Damascus plum."

On the way home along the lanes over the raised earth paths, past the white windmill shining in the flax, I thought "Poor little nothing. Poor, pompous locked-in little nothing. What's been done to him to turn him into this? Could he possibly have been born so? That might be even worse. He *shall* taste the Damascus plum. He shall" – and I rang up his aunts and invited Klaus to a Sunday lunch with us. "To luncheon," I said. (And think of that while you're weeding the lobelias.) "Luncheon, at 12.30."

They seemed puzzled and delighted. "How very kind. We don't go in for luncheon here especially not now with all the fruit. I'm afraid Klaus has been having rather a dull time. But are you sure?"

"Spotted Dick and Birds' then," said my husband, "Prepare him for school poor lad. Ginger pud? Kate and Sydney?"

"No. You'll see. Most certainly not."

"And do we produce a glass of wine for a fourteen-year-old or some coke?"

"Somehow I think wine."

"I'll buy it from the supermarket then. I'm not getting anything up for him."

"What about us?"

"Well all right. Maybe we'll need something drinkable to get us through. Why do we have to have him when you say he's dreadful? Nothing in life that interests him and he's fourteen years old. My God."

"There may be. Let's see."

"So, what are we having?" asked my husband en route to the cellar on Saturday evening, "You mean we're having fish as well as meat at Sunday lunch?"

"And cheese. And puddings. And I'm making tartelet things with pâté for before we start. Then the fish. Then the roast beef and York-shires as he's never known them and I'm doing a mousse of cour-gettes and broccoli with herbs, and good English mustard made with balsam vinegar, and gravy better than a sauce, with pheasant-stock and wine. And Bolivian coffee. And then he's staying to tea."

"Are you in love?"

"He is revolting. But I won't have him revolted. He's in England to learn, and I'm his teacher."

We had Cavell's little lemon soles hot and curly and crisp and light in breadcrumbs with lemons. Then we had sirloin of Scotch beef, not *en croute* but juicy inside and crisp on top with the green vegetables and little carrots with parsley and butter and chopped uncooked onion. The potatoes – Desirées naturally – I par-boiled and then shoved far back on the top of the Aga in hot olive oil. 'Extra-virgin' olive oil and when Klaus said "Excuse me what is an *extra*-Virgin?" and my husband said "Maybe it's a nun" Klaus laughed.

Out of the Aga came the Extra-Virgins like crunchy, golden soft-centred flowers. Then we had a red-currant water ice, the red-currants from Rusham. For the damson tart we had a jug of cream from Solley's Farm at Worth, thick and yellow, and the cheese was Cheddar. I'd spent a long time choosing it from five good ones. There was a local *chevre* and a perfect Double Gloucester.

The pastry for the tart was the best I ever made, I think. I'd iced the knife as well as the water and the bowl. It was crisp but flaky. Almost transparent. The damsons sat darkly inside it, basking in a con-gealing sharp-sweet lake of crimson juice sprinkled with hard brown sugar. They looked comfortable as fat black ladies in a spa.

On and on he ate. And we ate. He sat pink and absorbed and silent. In a final dizzy flourish I spun out into the kitchen and in a minute or so came back with a little pancake for him, filled with maple syrup. It rustled as it slid on to his plate.

We'd asked him if he'd like half a glass of wine with the beef and he drank two full ones, slowly and seriously.

"Chassagne Montrachet," he said to my husband, "Thank you", and pronounced it very good. "Very like a Riesling." My husband said, "If you were not fourteen years old I would offer you half a glass of Barsac with the plums," and Klaus said, "Thank you. I should like that. I don't think my age matters. My father taught me to drink wisely. He was a wine merchant."

"But surely – didn't he die some years ago?"

"Yes, I was nine. I suppose I'd better walk home. I shall have to cool off before Plum Cottage."

We walked first though along the sea-front a little and looked at the navy-blue line of France that meant rain was coming. I said that France seemed to be making some sort of statement to us and Klaus said, "Ah, it is a metaphor?" but didn't seem much interested in what that might be. He said soon, "Did you mean it that I might stay to tea? I've never had an English tea."

"What was your mother about?" we asked.

"She was a gardener, too," said Klaus.

For tea I had more than intended him to stay. I had exerted myself – we had small thin triangles of rye bread and butter, small thin triangles of white bread and butter, scones with home-made strawberry jam, in a glass jar with the strawberries hanging whole and suspended like rubies. We had Sally Lunn and Sad Mary and a gingerbread and a sponge cake with white icing, and fresh lemon-curd tarts and raspberry tarts the size of a fifty-pence piece. We had an English Swiss roll with black chocolate butter filling in it – not sickly black cherries. And – bother the boy for it had taken five hours and I'd only done it because it is so difficult – we had a Lenten Simnel cake soaking with fresh soft marchpain, soft as honey, light as air.

And somehow we got him home to his aunts.

"You are of course mad," said my husband, "but at least there is now one Swiss in the world who won't forget that the English can cook. It's a blow struck for international relations. Whether he'll pass the Common Entrance of course is another matter."

But he did pass. There was a miraculous option in the essay paper, *The Pleasures of the Table*. As far as we could make out he simply set down a number of esoteric and interesting recipes and gave a short treatise on wine. The examiner must have been his fairy godfather and must also have been somewhat surprised. The aunts and the uncle sent me an enormous pot plant with my fees and Klaus wrote a very correct letter. We kept in touch for some years until, as happens, we were down to Christmas cards when we remembered, and then to nothing at all. We forgot each other. But last year in Geneva we read in the newspapers that Klaus had been appointed a

Cantonal Judge and the news was too tempting to ignore. We wrote our congratulations and almost by return we were invited to dine with him.

And oh, such a benign and ancient man came forward to meet us, with the manner of Methuselah though of course much younger than us. He was tall, wide, pale, portentous, very slow and dignified in speech and movement and with a voice light and tiny as a gnat's – and as sorrowful as God. He and his wife took us to the very best of Genevois restaurants where the menu my husband said (afterwards to me) was particularly Swiss: short, rich and unadventurous. The wine was like the whites of St Nicholas-at-Ash – but when we said so Klaus only gave the small smile I suddenly remembered.

We thanked profusely, and Klaus's round-faced wife said what a pleasure it had been for them to entertain us. How lovely it must be for us to travel she said. They never went anywhere. How pleased we must be to get away from the English weather and the food.

"Of course, it's only what one hears," she said. I waited for Klaus – I watched and waited for Klaus – to speak. It was a very long time ago but surely, surely he might remember. Some little memory might stir. The soles from Cavell. The Elysium Yorkshire puds. The tartelets, the Sally Lunn, the superb cheese, the pancake, the basking black ladies in their pâtisserie cradle. And such a doleful, hungry boy.

"Oh, but I remember many pleasant things about England," he said, "about Kent. There were some beautiful little plum trees – I think they were in your garden, Anne. A very good little plum. It ate beautifully. Not English of course, I am afraid. It was a plum from somewhere in the Middle East. I believe Damascus."

A MEDIEVAL PICNIC

T. A. LAYTON

Four years is a long time to cherish an idea; the time had now come for me to attempt to give my medieval feast in Three Cranes Lane. It was a lovely spring morning in May, 1946, when I hailed a taxi outside the Law Courts.

"Take me to Three Cranes Lane," I said to the taximan. "It runs off Upper Thames Street."

"Three Cranes Lane?" said the taximan, mystified.

"Yes," I said. "Three Cranes Lane – it is about the second turning down on the right in Upper Thames Street after you have passed Southwark Bridge."

"I know! I know! But – oh well!" And he started off.

When we got to Southwark Bridge I understood what he meant. From there to Cannon Street railway bridge, there was not a single house left standing.

"I get you now," I said to the man as I jumped out.

He gave me a smile. "I thought it seemed that you hadn't been here for some years," he replied.

I have just said there wasn't a single building left standing. There was one – with its roof off – and that, curiously enough, was Pannonia House, which I had noticed as being so handsome four years back; it was the only one in the area made of reinforced concrete. That made my quest easy; the feast would be at Pannonia House or nowhere. I felt a bit foolish as I went into the entrance; why should I want to give a party in a stuffy office just because that was where one had been given half a thousand years ago? But I didn't want to go back on the idea – a feeling of hallowed ground, or something like that, I suppose.

A man in a white coat approached: "What goes on here?" I asked, but it was a redundant question, for the smell of furs was overpowering.

"Furs and skins, sir," he said.

"Can you tell me the name of the Managing Director?" I asked.
He looked at me suspiciously. "What for?" he said.

This was *the* moment for feeling stupid. "I don't want to sell anything or buy anything, and I haven't called on behalf of a charity," I said, "but I would like to know his name."

The man was no longer too suspicious, but was doubly mystified. "Well, it is Milhofer."

That was as much strain as I could cope with that morning and, anyway, I somehow felt that the next approach should be by telephone.

"Can I speak to Mr. Milhofer?" I asked two or three days later, and a few moments later a pleasant voice came on the end of the line, and I again said my piece about not wanting to buy or sell, and could I come and see him? Seated in the office half an hour later, opposite an affable and very young man, I explained my errand.

"Mr. Milhofer," I said ponderously, "well over five hundred years ago, almost on this exact spot, five kings were feasted by a vintner, and now my idea is to try and reconstruct the feast as near as possible as it was and as nearly on the same spot as possible. Will you let me borrow one day one of your office rooms for this purpose?" I paused, took a deep breath hoping to Heaven that what I had said had "registered". I need have had no qualms, for he kindly treated the request as normally as though I had come to sell him (or buy from him) half a dozen skunks. "Come and see over the building," he says, "and choose the room that suits you most."

We went the rounds. One could see that before the blitz they had been magnificent premises. The building had been more severely knocked about inside than appeared from without.

"That's all," he said when we had finished the tour. "The whole of the second floor is open to the sky and there is no roof left on."

"May we go and see?" I asked.

A few minutes later we were standing in a vast room, on the top of the house, of which three walls were standing, while the fourth had been knocked away, giving the most wonderful view of the river and Southwark Bridge I had ever seen.

On a building opposite was an enormous sign with the word "NECTAR," and down below, being blown gently to and fro by the soft mild breeze which floated up from the river, were wild herbs and flowers which had been growing there ever since the space had been made available for them by enemy bombs. The spot was so ideal for the sort of picnic I wanted to give, the view so typical of London as it might possibly have been that, as I stood there, I was too excited to say anything for a few moments.

"There is a big room underneath this which might be furnished in time," said Mr. Milhofer kindly, for I think he thought my silence meant disappointment.

"The feast will be here," I said, "even if it snows."

The next problem was to devise a menu, to decide how many people should come, and ways and means of serving the food for them practically in the open air. I had to start reading things up all over again, for it was one matter to find out what the kings and Sir Henry had had in 1363, but it was another matter to produce even one of the dishes, and harder still to produce them on the rations allowed. Over the number of my friends to be asked I pondered for some while. It seemed to me a shame to go to the lengths to which I was prepared to go and only have a handful to the party afterwards, but, contrariwise, as the numbers went up so would the catering difficulties become more severe. Anyway, numbers couldn't be decided until I had found out what they might have eaten in the old days, whether I could get what they had eaten, and whether, having got it, I and my staff could cook it. Preliminary scouting round told me that, while I could get a swan if I waited and even a peacock too, the chances of getting it on the day of (or three days before) the feast were remote, and the man who had promised to get me thrushes and larks was a boozy old boy who could be relied upon to produce dozens of them, provided he could choose the date; but it was quite certain he could not produce them on the day that I wished.

With the fish, however, I had two staunch supports in Mr. Hennings, the Managing Director of Sweeting's and Driver's Oyster Bar, and Billy Wallace, a doctor friend of mine in Grimsby. There was only one thing to do, and that was to renounce the peacock and ask Eleanor to let me have the enormous bubbly-jock (he turned out to be well over 30 lb. when he was killed) who had helped his wives to produce such a vast quantity of eggs for us in the past two years. Eleanor agreed, and I arranged to stuff this with a duck, which in turn had been stuffed with a pigeon, and inside this I wanted to put a snipe.

.   .   .

My next job was to get a wine the colour of heliotrope or tournesole. Now, the whole point of this story would be lost if I do not explain that I had foolishly got into my head that this colour was a vivid Mediterranean blue.

"How do I colour a wine bright blue?" said I, accosting Professor MacIntosh, Dean of the London School of Hygiene, in one of the vast corridors of his domain.

"Why not use methylene blue?" he said, giving me a curiously malicious smile.

Along I went and contacted my friend Walter Bales, expert on the subject, who promised to let me have a couple of bottles dyed to my own personal tint. I took a bottle along for him to practise with, and while he was manipulating the test tubes and finding out from me the exact depth of blue I wanted, I asked him why the Dean had smiled.

"I don't know," replied Walter Bales, giving just the same sort of smile.

"Will this concoction do my guests any harm?"

"Definitely not," he replied in all earnestness.

He was quite right; the drink did no harm at all, but it gave us all a bit of a shock the next morning.

.   .   .

"What would be the perfect number to ask to my open-air feast?" I asked myself [next]. It would be a shame to kill the bubbly-jock for just a handful, but Young would have to carry down all the trestle tables and chairs in his car, and there was a limit to what he could do in a day's work. Eventually, trying to keep to a multiple of five, I decided upon five times five; but I simply couldn't whittle my invitation down to under the thirty . . .

As I said before, the amount of reading needed even to attempt the feast overawed me, and twice did I postpone the provisional date I had fixed. When I had sent out the invitations and there was no going back I felt deeply depressed. In June I had provided a banquet for the Prime Minister and 200 people for the London School of Economics' Fiftieth Anniversary, and had run two buffet suppers for 700 people, all within ten days, and had been warmly thanked for it, but that planning was nothing compared to the feeding of my friends at Pannonia House.

When I had finished my reading and had assembled the recipes for a number of dishes, I then had to decide whether they were makable and whether they would be good cold. For instance, as a pudding I wanted to put on the fig-and-beer *fritours* which I had discovered in one of the Harleian Manuscripts and had already broadcast about, but the staff dropped so many hints about their taste cold (hot, they really are good) that I dropped them.

Forty-eight hours before the day I had an urgent 'phone call from Billy Wallace, who told me to be at King's Cross at midday to receive a crate of fish from Grimsby. He'd done me proud; Miss Jones, who had had to wait eighty minutes for the train's arrival, found that she needed two porters to get the crate on the taxi.

When we opened up there were still no disappointments, for Billy had given instructions that, while all the fish for cooking had been beautifully filleted, one of each kind had been left untouched. I decided to cart all the whole fishes, on the day, down to Upper Thames Street, so that my guests, while they were eating through their fish course, could walk over and see how they looked when they came from the sea.

On the fateful morning the day was cold, and there was rain in the air; the whole fish looked drab and clammy as they came out of the frig., the piment (or spiced wine) which had tasted fine when I made it the night before now seemed insipid cold, two hired staff had failed to turn up, and one of the taxis, which had taken *twenty-five minutes* to load up, had a puncture. Another taxi had to be found, and while all the dishes were carefully being loaded the waitresses arrived, the fish lost its clammy look, and Young decided that he would just have time to heat up the piment and put it into thermal urns.

It was threatening rain when our little taxi convoy left Gower Street and started off for Southwark Bridge, and, when we arrived, there was a cold wind blowing up from the river; but I hesitated only for a second when all the staff asked me pointedly if I was going to use the sheltered room downstairs.

"In the open," I said, and the die was cast, for there was barely half an hour before my guests arrived, and the amount of carting to be done was enormous.

The only disappointing thing about the place was the rubble on the floor. Still, I supposed it was medieval. What did they have in those days? Rushes, to be sure. Well, there were no rushes. But then at banquets (suddenly I had got it) *they strewed flowers on the floor!* And down below were all the flowers in the world. I rushed down and started to cut and took the handful upstairs. Obviously I needed a helper; I took a chance and 'phoned Basil ("World and His Wife") Taylor, one of my guests, who was on duty that morning at the B.B.C. Yes, he said, he'd come right away and tear up bracken and wild flowers. And how he did tear, and we got down the last armful just as it struck twelve and people started to arrive.

I suppose that if the running of the whole foray had not caused me so much sweat I should not have remembered so vividly what all the dishes [the bill of fare is reproduced here] were like. As it is, I can even recall the order in which my friends arrived (Maurice Platnauer first and Jossie Cadell last; Mary Horder's summer hat nearly blew off; Carl Roberts kept his overcoat on; Major Seyd didn't, and got rather cold) and who liked what dish.

Oddly enough, the Mawmeny, which sounds foul to modern tastes, turned out to be far the most popular dish and quite a gastronomic discovery; opinions were widely divided on the fish (I thought the carp an overrated delicacy, but the catfish and dogfish both excellent), but even politeness would not allow my truthful feasters to enthuse over the Viande Royale, which sounded so scrumptious on paper but turned out so disappointingly insipid.

The three puddings were very good, but cold marrow is not recommended – even when cooked with mace.

That, I think, is all, save that as the meal progressed we all noticed a pleasantly scented smell pervading the food, which my guests kindly put down to the hot spiced wine.

But it was the wild flowers and herbs as they became bruised by our walking to and fro.

MENU

Boiled Conger Eel   Steamed Latchets   Braised Pike

Steamed Gurnets   Boiled Carp

Cat Fish cooked in Spiced Wine

Dog Fish cooked in Cinnamon

Turkey

*[This had been stuffed with a duck which in turn had been stuffed with a
powerful stuffing made of garlic.]*

Cold Roast Stuffed Duck

*[Stuffing here was of sausage meat pounded with hard yolks of eggs mixed
with dry currants, cinnamon, and ground mace and whole cloves.]*

Mawmeny of Chicken   Mawmeny of Duck

*[In this case the chicken or duck had been boiled in milk and sugar. They
had then been taken off the bone and the juice had been boiled up with
semolina, ginger, cinnamon and cloves. The shredded chicken or duck had
then been put back and turned into a brawn.]*

Cold Marrow cooked with Mace Bread

Chopped Date and Ginger Jelly

Chopped Fig and Ginger Jelly

Doucettes

*[A sort of highly spiced custard flan made of egg yolks: which have been
cooked in a "coffin" – medieval name for a pie crust.]*

Viande Royale

*[This was made by boiling together white wine, honey, ground semolina,
ginger, pepper, cinnamon, cloves, saffron, sugar and mulberries. The
instructions in the recipe are that care should be taken "that it be thick."]*

Extract from *Five to a Feast* (1948)

THE OMAR KHAYYÁM CLUB:

A LITERARY BROTHERHOOD

CHARLES HODGSON

"O, my friends, when I am sped, appoint a meeting, and when you have met together be ye glad thereof, and when the cup-bearer holds in her hand a flagon of old wine, then think upon old Khayyám and drink to his memory." With this splendid phrase, the members of the Omar Khayyám Club sit down to dinner twice a year, in spring and in winter, as they have done for the past one hundred years, to commemorate the immortal memory of Edward FitzGerald* and to drink the cup that the Master Omar himself has bidden.

That a dining club should exist for a century is strange enough; that through two world wars a social gathering should have continued or its memory been kept alive is really extraordinary. Even during the First World War – even with the menace of the U-Boat at its height – the dinners the club indulged in seem substantial feasts. Could, one idly wonders, the founders of this literary dining brotherhood have possibly imagined in 1892 that the tradition of drawings, poems and indulgence in literary music hall – the substance of these evenings of fellowship – would still be in existence in 1992? The mores of our time are different; the intellectual quality of the brethren and their status in literary and political life are not as distinguished as in those distant days, when reports of the diners' speeches were regularly recorded in the public prints; but the club still exists and the brethren still demand excellence from their speakers – and from the food, wine and fellowship too.

The three who founded the club in 1892, Frederic Hudson, Clement Shorter and George Whale, merely regretted that "their intercourse had become too fitful of late" and agreed, as they put it,

---

* FitzGerald's anonymous translation of *The Rubaiyat of Omar Khayyám* in 1859 was his masterpiece.

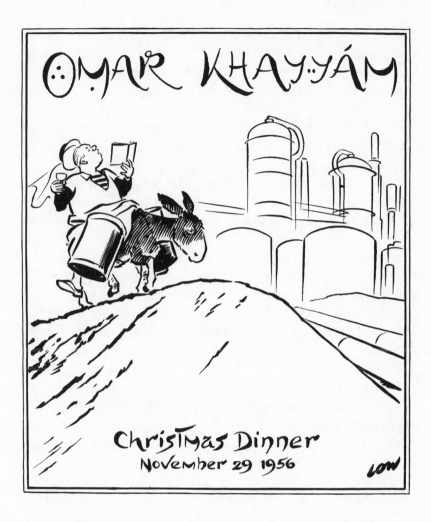

to combat opposing time and circumstance by dining together at stated periods. All three had known FitzGerald and, following Omar's injunction to appoint a meeting and be glad thereof, they asked a few kindred spirits to dinner at Pagani's restaurant in London on 13 October 1892. Among those present was distinguished litterateur Justin Huntly McCarthy, who was duly elected President of the sodality for one year. It was also decided to limit the club to 59 active members – 1859 being the year that Edward Fitz-Gerald had first published his enduring paraphrase of the Rubaiyat. The menu of the inaugural dinner was enriched by the pencil of one Arthur Hacker with a drawing of an oriental Bacchante, thus initiating the tradition, continued to this day, that talented draughts-men should year by year contribute to the evenings by decorating the menu. Artists have included Martin Hardie and David Low and in more modern times Edward Ardizzone, Ffolkes and Tim Jaques, and the drawings are of an often startling excellence. Also on that first menu was an elegant verse, and so the menus have ever since been en-livened by poems of varying character. The current member of the highest poetic achievement is John Heath-Stubbs, the blind poet, who has contributed works of real beauty. The verse is read at the dinner by the poet himself, and the drawing 'explained' by the artist.

Each dinner commences with the reading by the President of the Omarian 'bidding prayer', which voices the reason for the dinners themselves. The tables are called to order and the President invites a potential member to 'justify' – were such a thing possible – his in-clusion in the brotherhood. If he succeeds in so doing (and he nearly always does, for the bark of the brethren is significantly worse than their bite), the artist will then be asked to 'explain' the drawing that decorates the menu, and the poet called upon to read his verse. It has become the custom for the Secretary, who arranges the dinners, to intersperse the evening's proceedings with a verse of his own, to jus-tify his position as well as to warn of any forthcoming arrangements such as a 'Summer Outing' (wives and girlfriends also invited). The brethren are then invited to drink to the immortal memory of Fitz-Gerald himself: this will take the form of an amusing piece by one of the more scholarly members who has done his homework on some aspect of FitzGerald's work or life. Finally, a member of the club, skilled in the task, will put the guests to their proper purgation. It is the custom of the club that this speaker, rather than praising the guests, makes elegant fun of them. As the brethren will often have tried to bring not just their friends but the most distinguished people they know, the fun tends to be fierce. This speech is far from being bland, though I have never known a guest complain about the derision in which he has been held. It should be remarked, however, that by this point in the evening's sport all those present will each have drunk nearly a bottle of wine and the laughter and merrymaking of members and their guests will have caught fire accordingly.

Of course, these evenings will not always 'catch fire', nor will the verses and drawings always compare with the excellence of those

For I remember stopping by the way

To watch a potter thumping his wet clay:

And with its all-obliterated tongue

It murmur'd — Tamám Shud —

its Brother ray!"

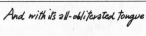

JAQUES.

مروت یا دز منفر گنه نی   ورمی وهمی گو سبتدی رانی
یا دیگری رشته درورانی   سیتی سپت کرد رضعب سالی

Here with a Loaf of Bread beneath the Bough
A Flask of Wine, a Book of Verse — and Thou
    Beside me singing in the Wilderness —
And Wilderness is Paradise enow.

early contributions. Times have changed: the novelists and poets of
yesteryear were much more clubbable than those of today, and
though the club counts many dons and lawyers among its members
there are now few litterateurs of the quality or eminence of the club's
early years. The artists are more usually cartoonists and the poets
versifiers, but the tradition is maintained and the ritual sustained to
the evident enjoyment of an eclectic collection of brethren, including
writers, poets and artists, but also politicians and businessmen, journalists and publishers, agents and advertising men.

Two books have been published containing the verses and drawings of the society's dinner menus from 1892–1910 and from 1910–
1929, and these can occasionally be found in antique book shops.
The names of the poets and artists include some of the most famous
of their time; and the members and guests read as a list of the great
and the good of the first quarter of this century.

For 25 years, Cyril Ray, the onlie begetter of *The Compleat
Imbiber*, regularly attended Omarian gatherings and was a brilliant,
if acerbic, after-dinner speaker. The quality of his contributions to
the evenings' enjoyment was marked by the enormous amount of

research he did for every speech he made. He believed very vigorously that, however frivolous, anything worth doing was worth doing well, and with fierce determination he demanded excellence of those who served the club in any capacity. It was a privilege to work with him, as his strictures were uncomfortable but just, and his praise was to be relished. In all the 24 years that I have been Secretary of the club, no-one else has given me cause for so much apprehensive excitement.

I trust there is still a place in our society for literary dining clubs of this kind, where the quality of the evenings depends on the wit and hard work of the club members to amuse and delight their fellows, and which lend a touch of colour and gaiety to life.

THE NEW REGIME

WENDY COPE

Yes, I agree. We'll pull ourselves together.
We eat too much. We're always getting pissed.
It's not a bad idea to find out whether
We like each other sober. Let's resist.
I've got the Perrier and the carrot grater,
I'll look on a Scotch or a pudding as a crime.
We all have to be sensible sooner or later
But don't let's be sensible all the time.

No more thinking about a second bottle
And saying 'What the hell?' and giving in.
Tomorrow I'll be jogging at full throttle
To make myself successful, rich and thin.
A healthy life's a great rejuvenator
But, God, it's going to be an uphill climb.
We all have to be sensible sooner or later
But don't let's be sensible all the time.

The conversation won't be half as trivial –
You'll hold forth on the issues of the day –
And, when our evenings aren't quite so convivial,
You'll start remembering the things I say.
Oh, see if you can catch the eye of the waiter
And order me a double vodka and lime.
We all have to be sensible sooner or later
But I refuse to be sensible all the time.

NOTES ON SOME CONTRIBUTORS

Kingsley Amis CBE, *b* 1922
Poet, critic and novelist (Booker Prize 1986). Contributor to *Compleat Imbiber* No. 2
(1958) and to second series (1986).
Robert Barnard
Read history at Balliol, Oxford, and spent 22 years teaching in universities in Australia
and Norway. He is now a full-time crime writer, sets crosswords for the *TLS*, and lives
in Leeds.
Asa Briggs, *b* 1921
Historian, former Vice Chancellor of the University of Sussex and Provost of
Worcester College, Oxford. President of the Social History Society and author of *A
Social History of England*.
Michael Broadbent MW, *b* 1927
Educ. London University. Writer, taster and auctioneer. Director of Christie's and
President of the International Wine & Food Society. Winner of the Grand Prix de
l'Académie Internationale du Vin (1984), honoured with the French L'Ordre National
du Mérite and the Gold Medal of the City of Paris. Recreations include playing the
piano and painting.
Wendy Cope, *b* 1945
Read history at St Hilda's College, Oxford; poet and former schoolteacher.
Cholmondeley Award for Poetry 1987.
Julian Critchley MP, *b* 1930
Conservative member for Aldershot; writer and journalist. Recreations: watching
boxing, the country, reading military history, looking at churches, collecting early
Staffordshire.
Jane Gardam FRSL (retired), *b* 1928
Novelist and short-story writer; winner of Whitbread, David Highams and Winifred
Holtby Awards. Married to David Gardam, with two sons and one daughter. Lives in
Swaledale, North Yorkshire, and Sandwich, Kent. Recreations: feeding, wining and
entertaining friends.
Andrew Henderson, *b* 1938
Educ. Salisbury Cathedral Chorister, Brighton Grammar School and Keele University.
Sometime wine bar owner. LBC Radio Wine spot with Bob Holness 1974-82. Member
of the Spanish Order of the Gran Orden del Caballeros del Vino. Past Chairman of the
Champagne Academy. Founder Member of the Cava & Penedès Wine Institute.
Charles Hennessy, *b* 1925
Author, *Nobody Else is Perfect*: memoirs of an advertising life in London, Paris and
New York. Recreation: sitting in cafés in France.
Charles Hodgson
Actor, Director of several film companies, including British Lion Pacesetter and
Oakhurst, and one-time director and publisher of several small specialist magazines.
Secretary of The Omar Khayyám Club since 1968.
Robin Howe, *b* 1908
Author of many books covering the cookery of the world; has lived since 1970 with
her husband on the Italian Riviera.
Bernard Levin CBE, *b* 1928
Journalist and author; Hon Fellow LSE; chief columnist, *The Times*; past-President,
The English Association.
David Lipsey
Journalist. Former Associate Editor, *The Times*; Deputy Editor, *The Sunday
Correspondent*; Editor, *New Society*; political adviser to Jim Callaghan and Tony
Crosland. Besides wine, likes opera, point-to-point racing, golf, and being with his
family.
Peter Luke, *b* 1919
Educ. Eton; Byram Shaw School of Art; Paris. Writer and dramatist who has worked

in the theatre, cinema and television, and in the wine trade. Recreations: conviviality, tauromachy.

Deirdre McQuillan, *b* 1957
A journalist who loves eating, she began writing about food five years ago when a friend asked her to help out on *A la Carte*. She has written for *The Independent, The Sunday Times,* the *Evening Standard* and, unintentionally, 'Pseud's Corner'.

Simon Murray, *b* 1940
Hong Kong businessman, author and ex-French Foreign Legionnaire. Recreations: collecting toy soldiers, running and squash.

Elizabeth Ray, *b* 1925
Magistrate, was social worker, cookery correspondent *The Observer* 1969-79, and contributor to various magazines and newspapers. Author of four cookery books and a biography of Alexis Soyer. Married Cyril Ray 1953. Contributor to *Compleat Imbiber* Nos 11 (1970), 12 (1971), and second series Nos 13 (1986), 14 (1989), 15 (1991).

Ruth Silvestre
Singer and actress. Author of *The House in the Sunflowers*, story of restoration of derelict farmhouse in Lot-et-Garonne. Contributor to *Compleat Imbiber* (second series) 1986, 1989.

Pamela Vandyke Price, *b* 1923
Educ. Somerville College, Oxford, and Central School of Speech Training and Dramatic Art. Author of 25 books on wine and/or food; 12 years wine correspondent of *The Times*; Chevalier de l'Ordre du Mérite Agricole. Winner of, amongst others, the Glenfiddich Trophy and gold medal and the *Wine* magazine book award.

Keith Waterhouse, *b* 1929
A novelist, dramatist and journalist who has written a wide range of work for the cinema, television and theatre. His newspaper column, now appearing in the *Daily Mail*, has six times won him national press awards. His latest book is a collection of his journalism, *Sharon & Tracy & The Rest*. Recreation: lunch.

Katharine Whitehorn
A columnist on *The Observer*, she has also done television and radio broadcasts, been on the Boards of the British Airports Authority and Nationwide Building Society and was formerly Rector of St Andrew's University. She is married to thriller-writer Gavin Lyall.

ACKNOWLEDGEMENTS

Articles and extracts have been reproduced by kind permission of the following:
The Lord Briggs for "Château Haut-Brion and the '89"
Michael Broadbent for "Great Tastings"
Jonathan Cape for "The Reluctant Host" and "Hollow-Hungry"
Wendy Cope for "The New Regime"
The Daily Telegraph plc for extract from *Albany* column
Duckworth for "A Medieval Picnic"
HarperCollins Publishers Ltd for "Fondly Remembered"
Charles Hennessy and Times Newspapers Ltd for "The Star-gazer's Guide" and "The Royal Ritz"
Bevis Hillier/Sotheby's *Preview* **magazine** for "A Visit to Mouton-Rothschild" and "Château Pétrus and the '89"
The Hogarth Press for "An Andalusian Tale"

The Independent for "Samphire Gathering"
Michael Joseph for "The Master's Brother"
Times Newspapers Ltd for "Paul Bocuse: 'God, too, is Well-known'" and "Good Burgundy is Rare: Great Burgundy Rarest"
Simon Murray for "In Partibus Infidelium"
Jean Redwood for "Not Much Silence in Court" (*Russian Food, All the Peoples, All the Republics* available through SPA Books Ltd, PO Box 47, Stevenage, Herts SG2 8UH, price £11.95)
Ruth Silvestre for "Sunday Lunch at Le Palissy"
Weidenfeld & Nicolson Ltd for "Bread Around the Mediterranean" and "I Think He was Killed"

Thanks are also due to the Omar Khayyám Club and Charles Hodgson for their permission to reproduce the three drawings taken from menus of the Club's dinners.

While every effort has been made to approach holders of copyright material, the Editor and publishers regret any omission from these acknowledgements. Apologies to any who feel aggrieved.